Calamari Polyticks

Michael Webb

Calmar Professional Publishing

Greenville, SC

Squid Pro Quo Press

ISBN-10: 0692278354
ISBN-13: 978-0692278352

DEDICATION

This is dedicated to the most delectable meal on earth – deep-fried calamari. When sliced to perfection with truth, traumatized with logic, and deep fried with reality seasonings, calamari becomes artfully delicious; a gratifying feast.

FORWARD

Common Sense Isn't So Common

Every now and again you come across something fun, original and thought-provoking. That's what happened when I was asked to read this book. Part biography, part satire and wholly unique is Michael Webb's perspective on what ails political *leadership* in our country (and perhaps the rest of the world!)

Deep down we all know that "something wacky" seems to be happening at the upper reaches of government, whether it's in the field of education, agriculture, administration, environmental protection, or healthcare, etc. "Why is it," we ask ourselves, "that whoever is *leading* (feel free to insert your favorite political group or corporation here) can't make basic decisions rooted in common sense?" Or, "Why do so many *leaders* often fall into the same self-serving role as their predecessors?".

Most of us are never in charge – at least, never in the position to make the decisions that affect many people - so we don't know what it's like for those in leadership positions. Michael does know what it's like to work through various jobs from the consumer side to the business side, and into various levels of management with start ups, small companies, and two fortune 100 corporations. [He created two products, patented one, and took them from ideas all the way through the business channels, (drawing board, manufacturing, production, distribution, sales, marketing.)] Over many years he has observed the performance of management, unions, and leaders across different fields at all levels.

But here's the point: Mike's strength is rooted in his common sense, honed through years of careful observation and broad decision making. Yet, he reminds us that leaders with such traits are as rare as a black and white television. Though the story he tells is mainly thought-provoking look at the political sphere, there is a scary truth behind it that is reminiscent of the issues that resulted in Frank Norris' 1902 anti-trust novel *The Octopus.* When you realize that over one hundred years have elapsed since that epic novel on human hubris, you realize that nothing has changed for numerous people in power. And you will wonder along with Mike, "Whatever happened to common sense and decency?" That is something *really* worth thinking about.

Steven Surprenant
(Aka: Nevets Tnanerprus)
August 2014

CONTENTS

ACKNOWLEDGMENTS

A sincere thanks to those who endured my shenanigans; the Surprenants, (especially Cheryl and Steve); Andrew Barton, the artist; Robert Cousins who edited and smoothed most of the bumpy structure; and the Premier Proof Readers (M. Blackwell, L. Campbell, C. Eure, and L. Seyedein) with additional thanks to L. Campbell for all that encompasses the electronic editing, formatting and layout.

This book could not have been written without enduring the daily monkeyshines of Central Planners and their politically correct, emotional, ideological followers.

PROLOGUE - PEERING THROUGH THE INK

There it was! A COLOSSAL SQUID (Architeuthis)! Ike had "waded" through his formative years to see one. Cruising in his bathysphere at three thousand feet below sea level, he spotted this elusive, mysterious creature! It was a

dominant presence living in an ocean full of little beings. Did the squid see Ike? Yes, because a squid cannot survive to maturity if it is not vigilant. If so, did he view Ike as a predator? Yes! But, why should a giant squid have to worry about a predator? The giant squid only has one predator – a sperm whale. At an early age a giant squid has to learn how to survive because it has many predators until it matures. It learns to swim (backwards) and to eject an ink cloud. This bewilders the predator which cannot see the squid because the cloud confuses the predator's understanding of its environment.

This scary beast has eight arms and two long tentacles; each tentacle possesses sharp hooks that grab prey tightly. The tentacles can extend twice the length (or more) of the arms. Their function is to expand quickly from the body, grasp unsuspecting prey, hold tightly and squeeze, while bringing the prey towards an arm loaded with suction cups. With its eight arms, the squid can capture many meals, using its huge beak-like mouth to shred the unsuspecting victims for food. Few potential meals escape its clutches.

The eyes of the giant squid are the largest in the animal kingdom - the size of basketballs - all the better to see through the shadows and surprise! If, by chance, the squid gets into trouble and the captured victim has its own razor-sharp teeth that sever part of the squid's appendage, that appendage will simply regenerate. With only one predator and many mechanisms of defense, ocean life is no match for it.

(As a nine year old boy, Ike had been fascinated with this creature while reading *Twenty Thousand Leagues Under the Sea*, by Jules Verne. Mr. Verne had written this creative masterpiece in 1870. Ike had checked it out of the public library and coincidentally, one year after reading the book, a movie, so entitled, was made. Ike begged his dad to take him. Although the year was 1955 and special effects were in their nascent stage, the movie was riveting for Ike. The giant squid was enthralling. Two years later, Ike had to write a report and give a presentation on a favorite book he had read. *Twenty Thousand Leagues*…was his choice and he received "best entertaining book report" as voted by his classmates.)

[Side note: Interestingly, a league was originally a measurement on how far one could walk in one hour. It is no longer a recognized distance but at the time of Jules Verne, a French league was approximately 3.5 miles. Indeed, 20,000 leagues (70,000 miles) was quite a depth, considering the earth is only 8,000 miles in diameter.]

Unexpectedly, Ike encountered many more squid. Knowing their characteristics helped Ike find them with ease. It had taken him 25 years of scrutiny of which he spent 4 years and $50,000 just building his bathysphere! The risk was enormous. The water pressure equally so. He calculated that for every 33 feet a person would descend below the water surface, the pressure in pounds per square inch (psi) increased by a factor of 14.7. If he descended to a depth of 3,000 feet, the pressure on his bathysphere would be 1337 psi. All this to chase an elusive, almost mythical creature? No! It was the process he was after! What Ike learned along the way, in addition to his encounter, was invaluable. These special squid are almost larger than life.

Suddenly, Ike had an epiphany. There are giant squid above water as well! It's just that they look different. They aren't as menacing-looking on land as they are in the ocean, but they are more deadly than their aquatic equivalents. What do they look like? How do they act? What are their maneuvers? What renders them so deadly? The physical characteristics of these squid-like land dwellers belie their real motives.

They can spot you from the shadows, look you in the eye with deep sincerity and empathy, grasp you with their oratory, spew colorful, rhetorical ink, then rapidly swim away, while stating they are simply "here to help."

What is "giant" about these land squid is not their physical size: It is their ego and the subsequent havoc wreaked upon their environment. They can spot you from the shadows, look you in the eye with deep sincerity and empathy, grasp you with their oratory, spew colorful, rhetorical ink, then rapidly swim away, while stating they are simply "here to help." The land squid's tactics work magnificently on those whom it deceives, because the deceived are unable to penetrate its beautiful and verbose rhetoric, its best tools of deception.

In the distant past, a giant squid somehow laid eggs on land and these eggs evolved into special life forms. These unique descendants had the instinctual characteristics of their evolutionary parents – the giant squid. On land, however, ink does no good to confuse because it cannot disperse as it does in water. Nevertheless, verbosity on land evolved to become an excellent surrogate for ink. Without question, verbosity is the gold standard for confusion on land.

Unfortunately, if students are not schooled in the rigors of math, science, logic and the scientific method, verbosity easily clouds their thinking, and they have no clear way to find truth. Incidentally, beautifully artful rhetoric takes much less effort than verbosity on the evolutionary scale of confusion, and the composer of this stunning rhetoric is held in high esteem for his charming compositions, meaningless as they may be.

Ike and a small percentage of others were able to carve through a deceiver's hollow grandiloquence because they had developed discernment using common sense, cultivated over time, by observing, experiencing, and applying what they had learned to life's situations, enabling them to see confusing issues clearly. Much of Ike's knowledge was built by reflection, parlaying self-taught disciplines with assimilation in the context of lived experiences. At times Ike had stumbled badly on life's path through his formative years but he learned to persevere despite the errors. Learning difficult lessons can be grueling. Fortunately, Ike and his buddies had formed a club as young adults – "The Gumshoe Truth Seekers" – where issues of the day were debated, honing their skills to slice through verbal smokescreens, drilling down to the truth.

He noticed that we all travel in metaphorical bathyspheres known as "terraspheres" above water, from birth to death. His keen interest in "what lies below" progressed while studying the physical sciences and the scientific method. Biology, comparative anatomy, botany, parasitology, astronomy, chemistry, and physics had become his terraspheres. These subjects became the backbone for his disciplined thought, granting him the knowhow to approach and dissect a problem. Ike recognized that his innate clarity of thought coupled with various devices to help peer through the "ink" would hasten his quest for truth. Social sciences and the fine arts provided counter points to the rigors of "hard science" and were a wonderful counter-balance to structured thought.

Most of our terraspheres today have very small windows and individuals peer through these windows with polyopia clouded by various colors of ink. In fact, most individuals do not know how to look or what to look for when dissecting an issue. Their vision is clouded. They cannot see truth or reality, and sadly, many are too lazy to make the effort. Why struggle? Struggle takes determination and discipline. As a result of his awareness, Ike recognized that countless people enjoy being spoon-fed because it is easier than feeding themselves.

> *We think we elect politicians to represent us, to work for us. Instead, we become their prey and work for them; central planning is their primary method of control.*

Television is an excellent example of spoon-fed entertainment that is highly addictive for many. Everything has been prepared for the spectator. All a person has to do is press the remote button, keep his eyes and ears open, and he becomes beholden to centrally prepared entertainment.

A major concept occurred to Ike after his encounter with the giant squid. The creature metaphorically resembled a "Central Planner." Central Planners are partisan, political giants who wish to control most facets of our lives. They spew beautiful ink, snare us with their rhetoric, squeeze us so tightly there is no way to escape, shred our thoughts through political correctness, devour our beings, and swim away backwards unscathed (always facing us!) Nothing sticks to them. Their slimy coats are superior to Teflon®. We think we elect politicians to represent us, to work *for* us. Instead, we become *their* prey and work for them; central planning is their primary method of control.

Ike recalled his first, real work experience when he was fifteen and the values it brought him. He had just finished reading a seminal work: *The Road to Serfdom*, written by F.A. Hayek, an Austrian born economist and philosopher, given to him by his boss. His boss had struck up a friendship with Ike and rightfully so, because he could see that Ike's values and ethics were identical to his. The rules and regulations of a position within the Central Planning Bureau of the state led to his boss's resignation from the state, and the establishment of his own business, fittingly named – "The Flea Marketplace." Ike enjoyed his job at The Flea Marketplace where goods and services were bought, sold, and bartered with whatever the buyers and sellers could negotiate among each other, not through a Central Planner, a fiat currency, or a third party.

That is one of the main messages within *The Road to Serfdom*: Centralized Planning demands that the will (whim) of a Planner, or a small group of Planners, be imposed upon the population and it utilizes effective propaganda to implement its will. Successful propaganda leads the population to a belief that the Central Planners' goals are the same as that of the population. Ike recalled Hayek's quotation: *"While the last resort of a competitive economy is the bailiff, the ultimate sanction of a planned economy is the hangman."* *(1)*

This Central Planning,-third-party-propaganda-generating mentality would appear to Ike throughout his life in various forms: Politics, education, media, and health care, to name a few. Even some organized religions succumbed. Unlike many of those within the population, who became spoon-fed into a lemming-like passivity, Ike's self reliance, discipline, and hard work, shaped his skills and galvanized his judgments.

> *"While the last resort of a competitive economy is the bailiff, the ultimate sanction of a planned economy is the hangman."*

1 IKE THE YOUNGER

𝕴𝖐𝖊 entered this world (1944) known as a "war baby" meaning birth occurred during World War II. Ike welcomed a brother three years later, and a sister, five years after that. It was a modest, middle class family. His mother and father grew up during the Great Depression and everything had value: Education, family, spirituality, teamwork, integrity, work, money, etc. WWII enhanced the appreciation of these values and because of this, Ike's parents' generation became known by many as the Greatest Generation. What great role models parents from this time period became. They persevered through the Great Depression and WWII, emerging stronger than ever.

One of the best lessons Ike and his siblings were taught was the value of discipline. It was instilled in many ways but one of the best avenues was through learning a musical instrument. This meant lessons, practicing, paying teachers, practicing, giving recitals, practicing, purchasing music, and practicing some more.

Ike's instrument was the piano, his brother's was the trumpet, and his sister's was the violin. Each became proficient in his or her instrument and to this day music is a large part of their lives. Ike's brother became one of the best trumpeters in Kentucky and Ike's sister took her violin to one of the pinnacles of music,– The Juilliard School, then on to a chair in the New York Philharmonic Orchestra. Playtime was never permitted until at least an hour of practicing was accomplished first. Discipline at its finest!

Another lesson taught was the value of money. Ike learned to deny an impulse purchase for the future reward of savings. His dad made his children earn money by working for it, and on Saturdays they would all visit the local bank with their passbook savings in hand to deposit what had been earned. (Einstein was correct – "…compound interest is the greatest mathematical discovery of all time…") No one can find his exact words or where the quotation originated but that doesn't matter. The lessons of work, discipline, savings, and earning additional funds through saving are priceless.

Ike and his friends were alike in many ways. They were taught these same lessons and values.

Ike recalled an incident with his dad regarding a penny; one single penny that makes no difference. However, pennies do make a difference as Ike learned. One day, while walking with his dad, Ike saw a penny on the ground. He stooped over, picked it up, rotated his body 90 degrees and threw the penny at a sign fifty feet away. Bam! He hit the sign squarely. "Dad! Did you see that? I hit the sign, right in the middle." "Yes, I saw it, but where is the penny?" Ike couldn't find the penny. His dad asked him to sit down for a moment to discuss the value of money. One hour later the lesson was complete. Ike remembers his dad's famous words at the end of the lesson – "Mind the pennies and nickels and the dollars will take care of themselves."

Another lesson was respect for authority. To respect authority was something that was understood. It was automatic. When a child or adult became discourteous, Ike was appalled. His friends felt the same way. He remembers discussing this with them numerous times. It was okay to disagree, but state your case factually and respectfully. Be polite throughout the process.

Speaking of politeness, decorum was taught daily and repetitively in Ike's house. Learn the words please and thank you, open doors for people, walk on the outside of the sidewalk when walking with a girl or woman, show respect for the elderly, offer your seat to the elderly, chew with your mouth closed, don't slur your words, speak clearly, stand up when a woman enters the room, show respect for the U.S. Flag, it's ok to be a little early but always be on time, be considerate, learn tolerance, choose your friends wisely, sit up straight, etc. Ike's friends were taught the same.

On Saturdays, Ike would take a city bus downtown to the YMCA to swim, then after swimming he would continue on to the city museum. He was ten years old. One day, the bus was more crowded than normal and an elderly couple got on the bus. There were no seats available. Ike got up from his seat and politely asked the man next to him if he too, would give up his seat for the elderly couple. The man was somewhat reluctant at first but it was a brief reluctance. He got up and the elderly couple sat down, side by side. The man looked ashamed but eventually leaned over to Ike and thanked him for setting a good example. Decorum was alive and well and so was gratitude.

2 HEEDLESS TO REALITY

𝕴t was a deep, congested, repetitive cough that Dr. Nicholas O'Tien (Dr. Nick for short) was spewing all over his exam room when Ike's pulmonary X-ray was taken. Dr. Nick was a respected pulmonologist, specializing in mesothelioma and black lung. He could read an X-ray with the best of them. Ike was only fifteen at the time when he visited Dr. Nick for a routine X-ray procedure. He had been taught to respect elders and offer assistance when necessary, so Ike offered a tissue as Dr. Nick reached for one, and a pack of cigarettes tumbled out of his shirt pocket. He hurriedly replaced the pack and excused himself for a few minutes. Ike saw Dr. Nick light up a cigarette outside of the office window and smoke it, quickly generating so much smoke that it obscured Dr. Nick's vision, inhibiting his sight to step back through the door. Ike wondered why a health care professional, specializing in pulmonary diseases would be a smoker? If anyone should know better, Dr. Nick should!

The evidence that smoking produces adverse health effects was overwhelming! Dr. Nick had a severe smoker's cough and yet was a pulmonary expert for everyone but himself. Ike was mindful of being respectful to elders but decided to take a huge gamble and asked the doctor why he smoked. Dr. Nick admitted that smoking was bad but it was his "only vice." It also helped him during a crisis and tasted good with a beer. Besides, he had planned on quitting after the holidays.

Ike grasped the situation immediately. He wouldn't have thought this was possible for a pulmonary specialist to be a smoker and from someone his parents taught him to respect. "Even highly educated professionals will deny reality and convert truth into make-believe through their own mechanism of idealistic propaganda," he thought. Reality and truth eventually become known, however, not necessarily to onlookers, but to the individual who fools himself. Ike paused for a moment then pondered further, wondering how extensive this was, converting truth into make-believe. His instinct was that it was pervasive. (This was continually confirmed over the years once Ike entered the private sector workplace after graduating college. His Gumshoe buddies frequently verified Ike's conclusions by comparing notes with one another, discussing the strange phenomenon of people being capable of denying reality.) The incident was profound and caused Ike to begin his quest for answers to life's events that heretofore he had accepted blindly.

3 MODULES IN HUMAN BEHAVIOR

𝕴𝖐𝖊 spent the next four decades learning the ways of the world. College, marriage, rearing children, earning a living, establishing a work ethic, relying on what he had been taught while young, learning from foolish mistakes, and giving things back to humanity (time, advice, and money). The fifth decade after high school was spent reaping rewards from diligence, hard work, and determination of the previous forty years. Many of his friends did similar things, especially his three Gumshoe buddies; they were from solid, disciplined, moral families. As each decade passed, notes were compared casually at reunions with classmates, but the true friendships made in high school and college were genuine, stood the test of time, and remained robust forever. That is not to say that everything was idyllic, especially throughout college.

> *Politicians, by their nature, are egotists with one reason for living: Ensuring their own re-election. This is done through rhetorical bluffing.*

If ever there were a movie to describe Ike's experience with college life in a fraternity, it would be "Animal House." Ike and his buddies experienced "Animal House squared." Was it immature? Absolutely! Did the Gumshoes finally settle down? Yes! Were hard lessons learned along the road to maturity? You bet!

Unlike the classroom, many of Ike's experiences at the poker table were invaluable: Learning how to play a hand, how to bluff, and sniffing out a bluff - particularly sniffing out a bluff. Once one can assess probability, sniffing a bluff at the poker table is the determining factor of success or failure. The same applies to real life, whether it be business or when dealing with the curmudgeons of calumny, political Central Planners. Actually, with those two skills fully developed, (probability assessment and the "sniff") it is easy to see the truth. Politicians, by their nature, are egotists with one reason for living: Ensuring their own re-election. This is done through rhetorical bluffing.

Poker, and to some extent bridge, became Ike's "night classes." The same was true for some good friends - Bat, Worm, and Goat, although not as extensive as Ike. (Strange that Gator, Bat, Worm, and Goat happened to be best buddies, living in.......Animal House!) Throughout the seventies, eighties, nineties, and Y2K, they would reminisce about day classes versus night classes, always comparing notes about how reality was so elusive to many. They agreed that lessons learned in the night classes, in conjunction with their formal education, helped them immensely in real life. The following example is a real life situation involving the poker read and sniffing the bluff.

Ike had an interesting issue in the seventies and early eighties where he worked as a pharmacist for a Fortune 100 corporation. Prior to his being employed there, a union of pharmacists had formed. A few disgruntled pharmacists swayed the majority to vote a union into collective bargaining control. Upon employment with the company, Ike had to join the union because the state was a "closed shop." It was mandatory.

How could this be? Was not freedom of choice a consideration? No! The Central Planners managed to put through legislation and made the state a closed shop. Ike found himself paying dues to a very unprofessional union (retired meat cutters) with which the pharmacists had affiliated. He attended his first meeting of the union members soon after he was hired and could clearly see that emotional rabble-rousing was a tactic used to keep everyone stirred enough into believing that the union was "for the good of all." It was eye opening!

Sadly, the conduct of the union leader and many of its members was deplorable. His first professional work experience found him peering through the "ink" of emotional rhetoric by the local official, which meant nothing regarding truth and logic, to the majority of his fellow pharmacists, but they thought it did. Ike never went back to the hall. He just paid his dues and resented someone else speaking for him but he couldn't change anything as a single member, especially as a new employee. The local official was a superb politician. He could razzle-dazzle most of the pharmacists using emotionally charged rhetorical ink.

Two years later, a strange twist of events occurred. Ike was made manager over all the pharmacists in the district where he worked. He realized, over time, that if the weakest link is protected by the union, all are protected, and protection is accomplished through emotional manipulation because the real issue was money. It was all about money. Union dues were paid to a union official who knew nothing about pharmacy, retail management, inventory control, prescription drugs, etc. But the official could spew ink with the best of them. Ike cleaned up the district, whittled through the weak links, replaced them with driven performers and eventually the union was decertified. Throughout the process, Ike was falsely accused of many things and had to appear before the (National Labor Relations board) NLRB. Two full days of testimony by deposition, and Ike was found innocent of all charges. Through all the adversity and perseverance, truth was victorious.

> *Ike clearly saw how collective bargaining rewards underachievers and temporarily soothes the majority, but punishes high achievers because the pay rate is the same for all.*

Many lessons were learned, especially around the negotiating table, (which resembled a poker table to Ike), facing union officials, asking for the moon regarding salary demands. Their bluffs were easy to read! These experiences were invaluable and applicable to most situations in business, education, collective bargaining, corporate bodies, communities, and of course, politics.

Fortunately, Ike had hands-on experience with these lessons from each "side of the fence" from early adulthood. Union negotiators would appear two weeks before contract expiration, rabble rouse the members, have a list of demands, but only one demand mattered: Pay increase. Pay increases were locked-in for two years, had nothing to do with performance, and if the pharmacists got a pay increase, the union dues also increased. Pyramid marketing, anyone?

Ike clearly saw how collective bargaining rewards underachievers and temporarily soothes the majority, but punishes high achievers because the pay rate is the same for all. Furthermore, incentives to produce higher achievement eventually diminish, thus reducing business efforts toward average performance.

He decided to keep a notebook of his experiences after surviving the ruthless attacks on him personally throughout the collective bargaining and decertification process, periodically adding thoughts and referring back to certain pages. Common themes reappeared throughout the notebook that Ike would consult periodically and their reemergence helped clarify otherwise cloudy issues wrought from the purveyors of meaningless magniloquence and emotion. Here are his initial entries:

- *Those that do not work, will work more diligently to avoid it than do it.*

- *Beware of anyone with power, especially absolute power.*

- *Most of the time emotional speech creates followers and trumps reason.*

- *There is a percentage of humanity that wishes to control the majority; this same percentage reveres other controllers (friend or foe) who secured control because it is the end (power and control) that they worship and any means to achieve the end is overlooked or permitted by a controller.*

- The highest personal accomplishment for a controller is control, not decency, integrity, or values.

- Followers of controllers emulate those they follow and are just as dangerous.

The other Gumshoes - Bat, Worm, and Goat had similar experiences in their respective work environments as Ike, and occasionally the Gumshoes would contact one another to discuss the experience *du jour*.

Worm decided to take a teaching position after college and his mien took on all kinds of contortions, mentally and physically, from his work experiences. Teaching high school was short-lived for him. Unfortunately, he taught at a high school which (it could be said) was a precursor to Chaos High, appropriately named Harbinger High School, because the Central Planners had not fully sold their "wares" into it; only partly, which was still a bad dream.

One policy replaced another before the replaced one was given a chance to succeed or fail. "New Math" was conceived and required to be taught, replacing the math that had been taught for 200 years. Spelling was to be taught by memorizing the word, not by phonetically sounding it out.

Bussing students was another matter altogether. Transporting students from school to school was mandated by the federal government to ensure "equality of education," with no regard for distance travelled, age of the student, or the time involved with logistics. The school day ended for students at 2:30 pm but many did not arrive home until 4:30 pm…on good days. Weary students had to get up each morning much earlier than previously.

Central Planning was slowly eroding local autonomy. Not only that, the principle of Harbinger High, Casper Milquetoast, was scared of his own shadow. The students, parents, administrators, and lawyers had their personal agendas and he was powerless to stop them. Similar nonsensical experiences brought on by government control befell Bat as well.

Bat was a Finance Major in college with a minor in economics. All the Gumshoes understood "math relevance" and knew how to manage money, but when there was a specific math issue to be discussed, the Gumshoes relied on Bat. Bat would bemoan the banking industry because he had first-hand knowledge of its foibles. Ten years before the disastrous collapse of the Federal Savings and Loan Insurance Corporation (FSLIC), Bat foresaw that it was a terrible disaster waiting to happen. But for years, nothing actually happened.

Once Bat looked at the numbers of the collapse, he found that numerous policies of the federal government were put in place dating back to the 1930s. (Remember: Central Planners "know what is best for you," the community, your family, etc.). Some of the banking policies were well-intended; other policies lost their justification with the march of time. Finally, more policies were created to postpone a run-away freight train to financial disaster.

21

There were fifteen policies that contributed to the Savings and Loan (S & L) debacle, but the root cause of the catastrophe was the Federal Deposit Insurance. It was an unsound policy from its inception, and from an actuarial viewpoint could not be justified.

In short, all S & Ls were charged the same insurance premium rate regardless of how risky (or safe) the S & L bank was. To rephrase: deposit insurance provided by the federal government paid no heed to any unstable financial structure of the S & Ls. It was a picnic for irresponsible money managers with no consequences! Another way to say it: Drunk drivers could drive their cars anywhere at any time and were not penalized for doing so!

Bat saw this emerging problem even when he was new to the industry. Yet why didn't the Central Planners see it? No doubt they did, but they were careless because there were no consequences for their raucous behavior. The S & Ls collapsed and the taxpayer was invoiced for the deficits: Somewhere on the north side of $150 billion. ("I know what is best for you"). Known as the Federal Savings and Loan Scandal of the 1980s, we, as taxpayers, are still paying interest on the debt. These are just a few of the instances where the Gumshoes pooled their knowledge to see the truth.

Fifty-three years after Ike's visit with Dr. Nick, he noticed that human behavior had not changed. It was now the year 2012, and Ike was 68 years old. He had noticed numerous incidents over the years that reminded him of Dr. Nick's ability to deny reality and rationalize his actions. His mind went backward for a moment and focused on Dr. Nick's behavior on that long-ago office visit. He was stunned to recall this highly educated medical professional, who was destroying his body unnecessarily by rejecting the reality of what he had learned about medical care.

Ike decided to examine the current status of medical care from a factual perspective. Where was reality regarding health care? Was it the "reality" of Dr. Nick, or was it factual reality? (Actually, Ike had lived within numerous facets of the health care arena his entire working life, so his knowledge base was extensive).

4 VAMPY POLYTICKS AND HEALTH CARE

𝔓𝔬𝔩𝔦𝔱𝔦𝔠𝔦𝔞𝔫𝔰, especially Central Planners, are basically the same. They are ruthless and unrelenting in their quest for power and control. Ike remembered Dirktee Trixon, a politician who became so carried away by his selfish interests that he was defrocked of the Presidency. Trixon cast himself as a conservative Republican through staunch rhetoric. When it came to "I know what is best for you," however, he imposed wage and price controls. He also created the Environmental Protection Agency, an extended, burgeoning, out-of-control arm of Central Planning, hardly a conservative move.

There are some Trixons who become caught with their misdeeds, but many more that do not, not because they aren't dastardly, but because they are incredibly adept at covering their tracks with "ink."

Consider a vampire and how it lives and sustains itself: A selfish, parasitic creature that operates from the shadows but promises its victims everlasting life if allowed to bite. The vampire knows what is best for its prey and either attacks by surprise or convinces by seduction. Deadly for the prey, either way! A stake of truth through the heart is the only thing that can bring down a vampire, yet it is very difficult to accomplish. Parasites live off the living. That is how they operate and ensure their longevity.

Another example of a well-known parasite is a tick. (POLYTICKS is the term for when numerous parasites enjoy their meal together.) Ticks will extract blood from several sources, known as hosts. Many times the tick will infect the host who is unaware he has been contaminated until it is too late. This process is known as *polyticking.* An old-fashioned method that successfully removes a tick is one where heat is applied. Once the tick feels true heat, he will disengage and run for the hills quickly. The heat must be very hot and concentrated for it to work.

Coincidentally, a vampy *polyticksian*, Barq Pamma had honed his only skill (hollow rhetoric) well over the years and he was now the GIANT SQUID (Architeuthis) of all squids: Thee President. His signature legislation (massive, convoluted, and confusing) was the UCA (Unaffordable Catastrophic Act) known as BarkCare. Remember, Barq lived (and loved) to spend money. BarkCare was the contemporary "opiate of the masses" and just like all great *polyticksians*, President Pamma found a way to print dollars for his causes. The genesis of BarkCare was easy to trace.

It is important to note that a signature statement of propaganda was initiated twenty five years previous to the UCA by none other than Hillib Hamrod, a clever puppet master of behind-the-scenes manipulation. She sung "Health Care Is Broken!" repeatedly and it eventually became a rousing chant of Clint Billbong's followers. Its haunting libretto was oft repeated and ultimately became "fact." Once it became fact, then there needed to be saviors to fix it. Facts and figures were jumbled continually but because so much of the generation following Ike had no math competence, this was inconsequential. "Health Care Is Broken" sung to the melody of "Morning Has Broken" became number one on the charts. The ink was in the water, beautiful rhetoric covered the land and the voters were royally entertained. To hell with the facts!

> *...the doctors had slowly lost control of health care to insurance companies, lawyers, brokers, consultants, hospitals, and managed care organizations...*

Fortunately, Ike knew the facts and he arrived at a simple conclusion. Health care was not broken: The majority of the people were. Their "weight" (literally and in summation) continually overloads the delivery system. It is the cause célèbre of their inferior health, which in turn causes all kinds of disease states, masked symptomatically by consuming drug after drug after drug. Dr. Nick

O'Tien smoked heavily, had a terrible cough, and took cough syrup…because he smoked. Why not quit smoking and correct the root of the problem, not attempt to treat the symptom? Two thirds of the population is overweight (3) which creates conditions of diabetes, high cholesterol, and high blood pressure, so medications are prescribed that "treat" the symptoms, not the cause. Consuming all these medications makes for unhealthy stomach upset, so meds are prescribed for this as well. Why not lose weight? Ike reasoned that even though he was not a physician, it was effortless for him to diagnose the problem. Exclusively treating symptoms (medical rationalization) brought on future complications for the patient, adding burdensome "weight" to many existing disease states. What happened to the truth which was simple? It was behind the rhetorical ink, not in front of it.

Ike went further. Examining the delivery system, he found that the doctors had slowly lost control of health care to insurance companies, lawyers, brokers, consultants, hospitals, and managed care organizations and yet the doctor was responsible for the patient's health according to the aforementioned entities. He asked himself: Who assumed the risk with every patient? Who studied for years in med school? Who got the call in the middle of the night? Who diagnosed the disease? Who was at the center of every malpractice case? Yes, it was simple to figure out the answers. The docs!

The UCA was taking health care to a much lower level, usurping all the power it could gather in the process. It was going to be run by the state, policed by the IRS, and yes, Central Planning was in full control. Ike realized that it was not about health care at all. It was entirely about Central Control of the population and if Barq and his buddies could seize control of various sectors throughout the land, they would eventually have total control of it! The health care sector was over one-sixth of the economy (17.3%!),(4) but for those who could not relate math to real life, the ratio was meaningless to them. Beautiful promises would constitute their reality.

Health care insurance was originally set up to cover catastrophic, health events, nothing more. As time went on, everything on earth pertaining to one's health became included in health care insurance, for everyone. "It is now to the degree that the Central Planners wish to control health care and they have an unlimited budget to do so, via tax revenues through the health insurance carriers," Ike pondered.

Central Planners' answer to everything is to throw money at the "contrived" problem: The taxpayer's money. So much money has been thrown at the states for all kinds of reasons, that the states have now become dependent on the Nanny Government. This is totally opposed to America's construct; the founders and their wonderful document – The Constitution. Today, if the states do not comply with Nanny's wishes, they will not receive funding for their projects. Central Planning thus owns the states. Central Planning has thrown tremendous amounts of money at education over the years because "Education in this country is broken." Sound familiar?

Of course, Corporate America, in many ways, can, and has become a Nanny to its employees. Corporate America has been hoodwinked into believing the health care ruse. There is a simple fix for corporate America's health care dilemma – empower every employee to become his or her own shopper for health insurance. Current statistics show that nationally, it costs $8,000 - $9,000 per year per employee for medical, prescription, and dental coverage: medical being almost 80% of the cost. The fix: Give each full-time employee $9,000 and have them become the shopper for their health care coverage. This removes the corporation from being in the business of health insurance. Since excessive weight is the cause of most health problems, those who take care of themselves, exercise, and have discipline with good diets, would pay lower premiums for their health insurance. Those individuals who do not have discipline with their weight, diet, and exercise will find that they have to pay more for health insurance coverage because they are undisciplined. This concept has already found its way into corporate health care coverage for the smokers. In many companies, smokers have to pay a higher premium just because they smoke. Why should a non-smoker financially carry the smoker? Why should a disciplined individual carry an undisciplined one? They shouldn't, unless it is their individual choice to do so; not because a Nanny says so or because it is "just the way it's always been done." The undisciplined have caused massive stresses on health care; the Central Planners tell the undisciplined they have the solution for them; and the undisciplined elect/re-elect Nanny Claus! This system is doomed to collapse under its own weight, literally and figuratively.

Adopting this solution, Corporate Claus, would also be removed from health care, removed from being the Nanny, removed from all the paper work, and know their cost for the year on day one. As a result, the individual is empowered to tailor his coverage personally, and is not penalized by the cost of carrying those that want their cake and eat it too.

Ike had seen the cause of the problem, the resultant dilemma, and the cure. He muttered to himself, "Unfortunately, most people have to be awakened to their lack of discipline through their wallets, not by reality."

Corporate committees agonize over cost increases, slicing and dicing data, reports, etc. The truth is that health care, for a corporation, is a cost share between itself and its employees. The corporation can become the insurance company (self-insure) or they can "hire" an insurance company to (fully insure) them. Each corporation has a culture and through this culture it arrives at its solution to the problem of cost sharing for health care.

"Unfortunately, most people have to be awakened to their lack of discipline through their wallets, not by reality."

To solidify his conclusion that health care was not broken, Ike looked at two other sectors which are not part of the medical delivery system per se: Insurance brokers and health care consultants. (They were not part of health care because in the past, purchasers of health care were able to discern for themselves what they needed and were competent to employ math skills regarding costs).

Ike saw "ink" everywhere. With closer investigation, however, he noticed that the ink disappeared into thin wisps of vapor once reality appeared. His scrutiny illuminated the root of the problem: All that remained after the vapor disappeared was the broker's self serving, pecuniary interest! Ike heard the broker's sweet refrain to his client, "I will fight for you!" His mind went back to CHS and one of the candidates running for office. It was the same sententious proverb then as now: "I will fight for you!" It was Antonio Fallace who borrowed Al Sore's catchphrase and he had morphed from a lobbyist to become a health care broker. Clarity was there for Ike! Health Care brokers squirt beautiful rhetoric, cloud their client's vision, set up various "pathways" for themselves and are detriments to their clients who want their thinking spoon-fed to them.

A broker (supposedly) shops for health care coverage for his clients. The client has chosen him to help them. After all, a broker knows what is best. (Sound familiar?) Most brokers have never been part of the operational health care arena but they have excellent rhetorical skills and furnish beautiful looking reports, charts, and graphs that mean nothing in reality. Not only does the corporation pay them for their services, but so do most insurance carriers, third party administrators, and prescription benefit managers. "Brokers are analogous to lobbyists," Ike realized.

Ike's refrigerator failed and he replaced it with one of HIS choice. "Why would anyone send a third party on a mission to buy a new refrigerator for their home," thought Ike. "Each situation is different. The room colors are distinctive for the home, the size allotted for the appliance is unique, and which way the fridge door opens is important. Health Care is the same," he reasoned. "The individual should be the shopper, not a broker, CERTAINLY not government, and probably not the corporation."

When Ike turned his attention to another segment of health care as he had with brokers, and looked more closely at a gaggle of consultants, he found the same phenomenon: Lots of self-serving honking with these geese. As Ike would see later, the qualifications for health care consultants are on par with U.S. Representatives and Senators which are minimal. Again, he realized the charade. Most brokers and consultants handily rose through the ranks because they were good at political correctness, rhetoric, and feel good stuff; in other words, perfectly suited to the uninformed buyer. The fix was in (to help, to consult), the rhetoric was set, and the uninformed became victims.

A major portion of corporate health benefit assessment requires math skills by the buyer, which has now become rare due to the recent educational approach to math. A third party consultant or broker, full of beautiful rhetoric who appeals to an uninformed purchaser in charge of a health care benefit, holds all the aces. The unaware prey has no ability to see the ruse. It was not necessary for Ike to look further than these two examples for verification of his thoughts that giant squid permeate the health care ocean. Health care is fine; not broken. The docs, hospitals, and clinics know what to do and do it well. It's the undisciplined individual who is broken, preyed upon, then convinced they deserve treatment for maladies caused by their lack of discipline.

The periphery of people and organizations outside of health care, reaching into it (to help) actually enhanced its demise by acting as multiple tentacles of numerous squid. They choked health care to death, all because twenty-five years ago, Hillib Hamrod said: "Health care is broken!" Her statement became gospel, and the resulting peripheral pseudo-industries were created and the "fix" was in. BarkCare was going to wrest control, using the third party fixers to achieve his goal and grab greater power in the process. Before doing this, however, Barq remembered what had happened four years previously with prescription medication coverage (Medicare Part D) and decided to apply the lessons, tactically.

To set the stage regarding Barq's maneuvers, there were two major Central Planning parties, the "Isquierdas" known as the far side and the "Derechas" known as the not-so-far side. Barq recognized that each side was filled with professional chameleons who could change colors instantly. After all, he was one. The Isquierdas were generally the big spenders, or at least that is the way it seemed. Since each side knew what was best for the electorate, they always solicited for re-election.

There was a particular hybrid Isquierecha, a cowboy, who wrangled and cow-poked his way to the top, but he had to pull all the silver spoons and bullets from his jaws before he ascended. The extractions were painful for the many dangling "*shadtites*" hanging from his palette, and his opponent was a difficult apparition to deal with. Once atop the mesa, Dubious Bosh pushed through a plan - to *help*, of course. This cowboy seized the moment to engrave his own special kind of "help" into health care. (Seems like most Central Planners are very interested in health care....because it is so obviously broken).

Dubious Bosh grabbed the megaphone and decreed, "Prescriptions for everyone!" As the head of Central Planning, he herded the Isquierdas and the Derechas into his corral and convinced them this was long overdue.

"We've been saying this for years," the Isquierdas screamed. "This isn't your idea! You owe us because there were no WMDs like Colon Ozcopea said there were. He gave us a huge ream job and we went along with it." (In retrospect, Colon believed he was set up by Dubious, but he could never prove it. Colon's political capital and credibility went right down the tubes and he became the butt of many jokes. He adroitly changed political direction and slipped to the far side, periodically jabbing the not-so-far siders with his own meandering rhetoric.)

"Mission accomplished; meds for all!" Dubious proudly proclaimed. An Isquierda, who had camped out in a tent in front of a tattoo shop on Pennsylvania Avenue for a week to protest free meds, yelled, "You've said mission accomplished before, Dubious." Dubious smiled as only a cowpoke can, and replied, "You should be happy! You are going to get all your meds for free."

The Isquierda's retort was slow because he had to ferret out a notecard with talking points. As he reached into his left pocket and pulled the talking points card out, another card fell to the pavement. It was his Electronic Bank Transfer (EBT) card into which the Central Planners deposit funds for food every month. Sometimes the EBT provides great tasting fruit (out of season), cigars, and even a toaster oven. Another Isquierda grabbed the card and darted into the closest video game arcade. He blended immediately into the colorful lights of the arcade and disappeared; a veritable moving tattoo canvas because he was "painted" with all those arcade colors. The first Isquierda replied the standard response to any thought, "Whatever." He proceeded to read from his notecard and screamed, "You lied, kids died, Hurricane Katrina was your fault, and my disability check isn't the same as your salary. That's WRONG Dubious. That's not fair!" Although the protest wasn't coherent, it did not matter. Protesting incoherently was considered a high calling by the Isquierdas rather than not protesting at all even if there were nothing to protest about.

Ike knew the ruse regarding prescription medications, repeated historically – "You must take your maintenance medications to remain healthy." The word for this is "compliance." The truth, however, lies elsewhere. The real truth is you must keep your BMI (Body Mass Index) in a healthy range, eat nutritiously, and exercise regularly to remain healthy. Very few medications cure anything. Most medications treat symptoms instead of the disease itself. Tragically, the undisciplined take billions of dollars of medications to keep their cholesterol numbers in line and blood pressure values acceptable. Then they order a juicy rib-eye steak, a baked potato with butter and sour cream, a slice of double chocolate pie for dessert and take a nap afterwards. But they washed it all down with a diet soda.

In retrospect then, Ike had seen through the "health care is broken" hoax when it first began and he watched it evolve over time from hoax into fact. It was easy for Ike because he understood the squid and its methods and he applied this knowledge to the entertaining leaders who knew how to manipulate with their beautiful rhetoric. Ike noticed that Central Planners (entertaining leaders) all have the same tripartite code for life:

1. "I think, therefore, it is."

2. "I know what is best for you."

3. "Continue to believe me and re-elect me so I can give you what is best for you."

Central Planners are at their finest when sedating and trapping the uninformed, while simultaneously convincing their anesthetized prey that they must re-elect them for their future safety and well-being. A favorite catchphrase of a Central Planner is – "these are complex times with complex issues." Of course things are complex and

Central Planners are desperately needed by all to offer solutions and simplify the complexity for us. He referred to his notebook:

Never held accountable; always forming committees; let's do a study; humor their prey; never answer a question; never admit a mistake; excellent at the blame game; stay close to lobbyists; welcome chaos; keep 'em stirred, and whenever possible, tell them the issue is VERY complex.

5 NOITACUDE

𝕴𝖐𝖊 had recalled his thoughts, lessons, notes, and experiences from his life's events. He wondered if the educational system were decomposing as rapidly as health care. What better place to investigate than Washington, AC/DC? He decided to visit the nation's capital, which was expected to exhibit some of the best schools and programs across America since all of the Federal Central Planners reside there. Surely their professed code of "I think, therefore it is" and "I know what is best for you," will be proven?

He caught an inexpensive flight to Washington National Airport and quickly noticed how run-down and difficult to navigate it had become. Why have an airport this shoddy whether it resides in the nation's capitol or not, he asked himself. The answer came quickly. The Central Planners and their staffs all fly charters, private jets of their own, or those of lobbyists. A majority of their flying is back home to disperse goodies or on a flight known as a "Co-Del." Co-Del stands for Congressional Delegation; a junket of politicians (usually bi-partisan so that things look proper) that travel anywhere they wish, investigating anything they dream up. (One recent example: family, staff, and politicians flew to the Galapagos Islands

37

for a week to investigate global warming now re-worded as "climate change." Co-Del is political speak for vacation.) The airport was paradise compared to what he later found at the schools. He decided to visit a well-known, highly rated school – Bedlam High – and made an appointment with the principal.

Upon arrival at Bedlam High, Elsie Nowerk, the administrative assistant to the principal, let Ike know that the principal was very busy, had a full schedule of meetings dealing with very complicated issues, and could only spare a few minutes. After that welcome Ike realized he had some time to kill, so he spent his time reading the student newspaper, perusing yearbooks, and observing students coming in and out of the office. After a two hour wait, he was finally ushered into the principal's office.

"What has happened to this area and the standards of education?" Ike asked. "This is home base for all Central Planners who know best and want to help. It looks like a shambles to me. I saw poor facilities and students who cannot spell or add correctly. And I watched a school newscast in which no one knew the words to our National Anthem. But when I looked at numerous honor rolls, they all have straight As."

Peter Principal of Bedlam High, leaned back in his Queen Ann, silk-embroidered swivel chair, with imbedded, vibrating heaters, and said, "You are terribly mistaken. We have a fantastic high school because we have done everything the Central Planners have told us to do." He went on further, "Everyone wins here. We eliminated homework, let the students choose their subjects, threw away all red grading pencils, and we started taking educational field trips daily. When a parent interferes, we instruct the student to sue and that solves the situation immediately. This year, after fifth week break, we are going to bus in some students from Anything Goes H.S. to amalgamate them into our system." Adding more comments, Peter stated, "These are complicated times with complex issues, but we know what to do and how to do it."

Peter Principal expounded further, "The Central Planners permitted collective bargaining some time ago and the results have been fantastic for the teachers. They can retire with 150% of their base pay after twenty years of service, health care fully paid for, and if they served on any re-election campaigns, their retirement pay is 165% of their highest year's salary plus bonuses. Ninety-nine percent of all teachers received bonuses and they all worked on re-elections for Central Planners. Only one teacher did not, but he got full disability (145% of base pay) after fifteen years because he contracted an STD from the teacher who teaches Sex Ed."

Ike responded, "But what about the students? The teachers have wonderful jobs with outstanding benefits, but the future of our country lies with the students." Peter Principal rotated his chair counter -clockwise facing away from Ike. With a wry smile, Peter said, "The students will be guaranteed jobs within the government when they graduate. The best ones will rise to become Central Planners; the next best will be Assistant Central Planners; and the third tier will be teachers. Those jobs will consume all of our graduating students. No one will be without work. In fact, we have internships for sophomores and juniors that pay twice the minimum wage if you know any young person who would be interested."

Ike thanked him and beat a hasty retreat out of Peter Principal's office. Just then, Elsie Nowerk bounded through the door and exclaimed, "Peter! Your appointment for this afternoon's barbeque and golf outing has been changed to next week. The Central Planners need two full days for recreation and the only place it could be scheduled was Bimini."

Ike wondered how many of the Central Planners' children attended public schools. The answers are difficult to find because "ink" is everywhere in this town and backpedaling is a daily exercise for every Central Planner. (Even their exercise bikes only pedal one way – backwards.) The best figures obtainable indicate that six percent of Central Planners' children attend public schools, but that statistic is only from kindergarten to third grade. Remember, the entitled voters do not have math skills so they cannot discern whether these figures are meaningful or not. To them, what counts is "P.C. Speak" and as long as it is beautiful, all is well.

Ike delved more deeply through the "ink" regarding simple statistical data on the AC/DC public schools. It took him a tremendous amount of digging to get to the facts. A gentleman by the name of Adam Schaeffer had published a report (March 3, 2010) on costs per student in various metropolitan areas across the United States. The name of the report is *Policy Analysis - - They Spend What?* Mr. Schaeffer is a policy analyst with Cato's Center for Educational Freedom, a public policy research organization dedicated to individual liberty, limited government, free markets, and peace. (Cato is a "Think Tank" and is rated number six out of the top fifty think tanks in the United States). He is analytical in his approach, and the report is revealing. The reported statistics on public spending per student are always less than the actual spending. This is by design because it *looks* better that way. Why would the Central Planners not want to look good? They are all about "the look" and it is the look, not the reality that counts with them. Let's have a look at reality - what the truth is.

Per Mr. Schaeffer's article:

Although public schools are usually the biggest item in the state and local budgets, spending figures provided by public school officials and reported in the media often leave out major costs of education and thus understate what is actually spent.

To document the phenomenon, this paper reviews district budgets and state records for the nation's five largest metro areas and the District of Columbia. It reveals that, on average, per pupil spending in these areas is 44 percent higher than officially reported.

Real spending per pupil ranges from a low of nearly $12,000 in the Phoenix area schools to a high of nearly $27,000 in the New York metro area. The gap between real and reported per-pupil spending ranges from a low of 23 percent in the Chicago area to a high of 90 percent in the Los Angeles metro region.

To put public school spending in perspective, we compare it to estimated total expenditures in local private schools. We find that, in the areas studied, public schools are spending 93 percent more than the estimated median private school. (Emphasis mine).

Citizens drastically underestimate current per-student spending and are misled by official figures. Taxpayers cannot make informed decisions about public school funding unless they know how much districts currently spend. And with state budgets stretched thin, it is more crucial than ever to carefully allocate every tax dollar.

The following table is taken from Mr. Schaeffer's article and is self-explanatory. The District of Columbia is highlighted (emphasis mine).

State	District	Real Public Expense	Stated Public Expense	Estimated Private	% Higher Than Private
AZ	Cave Creek Unified	$13,929	$9,024	$6,770	106%
AZ	Deer Valley Unified	$9,365	$8,323	$6,770	38%
AZ	Paradise Valley Unified	$12,321	$10,734	$6,770	82%
CA	Beverly Hills Unified	$20,751	$11,205	$8,378	148%
CA	Los Angeles Unified	$25,208	$10,053	$8,378	201%
CA	Lynwood Unified	$11,215	$8,761	$8,378	34%
DC	District of Columbia	$28,170	$17,542	$11,032	155%
IL	City of Chicago, District 299	$15,875	$11,536	$8,849	79%
Il	Elmhurst, District 205	$15,205	$11,679	$8,849	72%
IL	North Chicago, District 187	$13,348	$12,959	$8,849	51%
MD	Prince George's County	$15,225	$13,025	$11,032	38%
NY	Great Neck Union	$29,836	$21,183	$10,586	182%
NY	Lawrence Union	$29,451	$17,359	$10,586	178%
NY	NYC-Chancellor's	$21,543	$17,696	$10,586	104%
TX	Houston Independent	$12,534	$8,418	$9,421	33%
TX	North Forest Independent	$12,719	$9,050	$9,421	35%
TX	Spring Branch Independent	$11,412	$7,816	$9,421	21%

VA	Arlington County	$23,892	$19,538	$11,032	117%
	City Average	$19,275	$12,663	$9,173	109%
	High-Income Average	$19,171	$13,408	$9,173	107%
	Low-Income Average	$15,221	$11,580	$9,173	62%
	Overall Average	$17,889	$12,550	$9,173	93%

Throwing money at a contrived problem is a Central Planner's solution because the money is not theirs, the results do not matter, and there is no accountability anyway. "Maybe, just maybe, the extra dollars spent per student in the public schools are worth it?" Ike

Throwing money at a contrived problem is a Central Planner's solution because the money is not theirs, the results do not matter, and there is no accountability anyway.

thought. So he tried to find the answer through academic performance, the measure being Scholastic Aptitude Test (SAT) scores. "This is difficult to find," Ike muttered to himself. He did find an article in the Washington Times newspaper from August 30, 2005 with the headline: "D.C. SAT scores lowest in the nation." He found a more recent article from the Washington Post, dated September 26, 2013. Melissa Salmanowitz, a spokeswoman for D.C. public schools is quoted, "Those from the District's public schools, regular and charter, had an average (SAT) score of 1200….far short of national scores."

Ike concluded that throwing more money at the education problem didn't help one bit. Scholastic performance remained horrible right in the back yard (under the noses) of those who know what is best and can fix anything because they always have solutions.

"This is merely high school and it is pandemonium," thought Ike. He made a quick call to Worm, now a full professor, to describe his visit. Worm was not surprised. The "fixes" for education which had begun nearly forty years ago, when Worm had his first job as a high school teacher, had now completed the circle of educational destruction. Worm verified Ike's conclusion that most high school students who have graduated over the past thirty years do not have the requisite math skills. Worm taught in college and he saw what the high schools produced. With little to no math competence, most voters who became eligible to vote over the past thirty years wouldn't pay much attention to Mr. Schaeffer's article because their ability to decipher it would be minimal.

Ike had to look elsewhere for a remedy. "I'll just take a quick look at public universities to determine if the system straightens the students out," Ike mused. It didn't take long to see this reality as well. Ike went online and noticed that many universities were fraught with meaningless majors and that costs were skyrocketing every year. Most schools' largest department was student aid-diversity. "That is very curious to me," thought Ike. "I wonder why?"

The answer turned out to be quite simple: These institutions have increased their charges for a college degree, because the Central Planners have declared "college for all...part of the American dream." They have thus become lending organizations to enable this declaration of the dream to become a reality, most of which is meaningless. Ike realized that it is the same kind of repetitive, deceptive hoax as the health care propaganda scenario. Proclaim health care to be broken so you can fix it. Declare a college education to be a right AND part of the American dream, create the need, raise prices religiously, and then lend money to the dreamers for worthless degrees. What a vicious circle! Ike was astonished that this deceptive technique of "You deserve the American Dream" worked every time with the majority of non-thinkers. Central Planners instinctively know this as well as how to get re-elected.

Ike had seen *NOITACUDE* (*EDUCATION* spelled backwards) for what it was, not what he was told, and the reality was harsh. The schools and teachers became surrogate parents for those students who had not experienced proper parenting in the home. The Central Planners had enabled this predicament by permitting an "anything goes" mentality to family care, because the parent (parents, if the child is lucky enough to have two parents) has no wherewithal to parent. That ability was removed by ill-conceived social justice programs creating dependence on the Central Planners through Touchy Feely, Nebulosity, History Redux and PC 451, the crusher of them all!

One teacher was responsible for baby sitting, instructing, disciplining, and analyzing thirty dependents (other people's children). He further concluded it was an impossibility to believe this can work. It is difficult for two parents in a stable environment to rear two to three of their own children properly. Since math competence has no meaning to an uninformed parent, the 30:1 ratio of children to surrogate parent doesn't worry the unapprised.

Ike expanded his thoughts and finally deduced that the multiple entitlement programs of perceived goodies have created a Nanny State of dependents partaking of those goodies from cradle to grave. The school system is just one portion of the pseudo-luxury cruise. Once the family unit is destroyed, the Central Planning Nannies assume the parental functions (nurturing, disciplining, praising, feeding, educating, etc.), and the constituency has become controlled and intimately linked to Central Planning forever.

He also noticed that the Central Planners' children attended private schools (for 2.5 times less than the cost per student at a public school), were accepted to prestigious universities (as legacies) and worked in well-paying private sector positions when they graduated. Many began their careers as vice presidents of banks or road building construction companies, although they had no experience in these fields. They had one huge advantage over most of their peers, however: They were connected to Central Planners.

Central Planners apply this same con to owning a house. Many who cannot afford a house (for what ever reason) are told they deserve it. Hard work, determination, disciplined savings, etc., have no meaning when "deserve" enters the equation. Central Planners arrange loans for them. They *help* them to the deserved American Dream. Before long there are numerous defaults on these loans and the diligent, responsible citizens pick up the tab, because the Central Planners raise taxes to pay for the defaulted loans. Ike recognized the ploy and he etched it in his head, thinking, "Get elected. Say what you have to say to fool the ignorant. Use other people's money to enable the ignorant to achieve "the American Dream." Repeat this cycle for whatever you wish to control."

6 MONUMENTS TO THEMSELVES

Of course Central Planners were always working hard at their own re-election! The entitled had no sense to determine truth; facts had no meaning. Indeed, most all Central Planners were re-elected. That is astounding but believable because reelection season is when they are at their best.

Ike sought to know what the qualifications were to run for U.S. Senator and U.S. Representative. "If these people are entertainers and this is a popularity contest, I'll bet the qualifications are minimal," he determined. "To spew beautiful rhetoric only requires one have that particular skill. So, where is the truth?" This is what Ike discovered.

A U.S. Representative has three requirements:

1. **Twenty five years of age**
2. **A citizen of the United States for at least 7 years**
3. **Be a resident of the state at the time of election**

A U.S. Senator also has three requirements:

1. **Thirty years of age**
2. **A citizen of the United states for 9 years**
3. **Be a resident of the state at the time of election**

[Side note: "Present" (as in gift), is a major portion of the word re<u>present</u>ative. In fact, represent (as in re-gift) makes perfect sense for this position.]

There was a committee chairman who determined how the Representatives (Re-gifters) would "represent" (re-gift) their districts. His name was Jerry Meander and he assured the naïve mushes that all was fair. (A mush is a person who has been filled with beautiful rhetoric and believes it, because he has no real ability to think for himself.) After all, when the enabled do not have a solid foundation to make a decision, Central Planning and its committees will do their thinking and deciding for them.

Jerry got his start in the carpet business, bagging small samples for potential buyers. It was an easy sale for Jerry because what he sold was promise, not carpet. He promised whatever the buyer wanted. Colors, customization, thickness, easy to clean, etc., were Jerry's hooks and did he ever pad things! He bagged carpet for years, padding his profits, and sold rugs by the truckload.

Once Jerry became elected, he applied what he had learned from bagging carpet, and formed a committee to ensure fairness with governance. One committee member would make a deal with an opposing committee member that had nothing to do with fairness, but Jerry wouldn't care, nor would the committee members. They would argue and spit when the cameras were rolling, but be best of friends off camera. The performers were entertaining, the entitled were yelling and screaming favorably, and the match was always fixed. It's a sell-out both ways: The entertainers were frauds and there wasn't an empty seat, was Ike's conclusion.

Ike decided to take a look more closely at a famous, corny Central Planner, just to see what he was all about.

"Cornelius! Cornelius Calvin!" his mother yelled. "I thought I told you to quit building statues of yourself and do something constructive," she exclaimed. "Besides, your sixth birthday party is tonight and you have to get in here to clean up." The only thing Cornelius enjoyed more than building statues to himself was a party. He could work his magic at a party. Corny knew at an early age that he could sway large groups of adults by telling them cute things and anything else they wanted to hear. He was a consummate entertainer and could not wait for his birthday party to begin that evening.

Some of his young buddies would be there, but he was more interested in adults, especially adults with power and influence. Corny would grow up to be one of the most beloved politicians (entertainers) ever! It did not make a difference which part he played: He could be a good guy or bad guy. He knew how to entertain, and thus, how to lead. As he grew into adulthood, he knew that most of the voters could not tell the difference between leading and entertaining, and therefore, he could do anything he wished as long as he was re-elected. Once in office, he worked his magic. With other people's money, of course.

Here is an example of his cavalier attitude. (Remember – "I think, therefore it is.") The policy of Corny's state was that a politician had to be dead for fifty years before a statue could be built and erected for him in the Capitol. Corny managed to wriggle an exception to the policy, and then suddenly became humble and appreciative when the statue stood before his eyes. In fact, Corny was memorialized (courtesy of himself) across his state more than anyone alive by highways, bridges, commemorative plaques, and statues. Cornelius Calvin Sale Jr., aka Senator Robert Byrd, ("Triple K" to many) of West Virginia, was truly a monument to himself.

Quite a tale for humble Corny Sale;

Use taxpayers' money to honor this male;

Bridges, plaques, parks and statues will be;

Proliferating everywhere for all to see!

7 THE INVESTIGATIVE PROFESSIONAL WRESTLERS

𝕴𝖐𝖊 noticed more universal traits of Central Planners. Just listen to them (if you can stand it) and they will tell you. The Central Planners always let us know how complicated and difficult a situation is. If an issue is portrayed as convoluted it must be so. Therefore, we need a Central Planner or a committee of Central Planners to untangle the convolution and lead us to a solution.

Additionally, he noticed that they always tell us how hard they work. There are many meetings that last far into the night. They make deals everywhere. They work hard because they tell us they do, and the media glamorize their activities.

> They work hard because they tell us they do, and the media glamorize their activities.

Ike flipped a few pages in his notebook and it revealed yet another trait. Central Planners pretend to investigate each other continually. It is all a play-act by the supreme entertainers. They say they will look out for us because they keep a very close watch "on the other side" (like one pro wrestler battling another, brawling for all it's worth). There are hearings, depositions, and committee investigations everywhere, occurring with great predictability and regularity.

It takes (seemingly) infinite amounts of time for these hearings. Days, months, even years are spent regarding good guy versus bad guy fighting for us in the ring of political correctness! There is quite a bit of scowling and finger pointing by these wrestlers, yet little is accomplished, no answers are uncovered, and there are very few punishments handed out for all these purported misdeeds. Each side will claim victory.

But just like the pro wrestler, "The Masked Cudgel," they can look bludgeoned when they are not (remember, their "make up" is fake) and the punishment for misbehaving is usually a slap on the wrist. Pro wrestlers are entertainers, not wrestlers. They scream and holler at their opponent (prey), appear to pound them into submission and the on-lookers pack the arena, also screaming and hollering for their favorite. Participants and spectators know it is a ruse. After the match, the opponents clean off the fake "blood" and enjoy a dinner together while counting their money garnered from the on-lookers.

Ike also discovered there were occasional resignations of the participants which deflect the spotlight from the true perpetrator. Once things die down, however, the one who resigned is reassigned to a better job within the Central Planning arena. (It is known as "resign for a better reassign.") He grinned and realized that no one ever gets fired if he is part of the collective bargaining unit within Central Planning. Promotions are easy, work is easier, salaries are enormous, and expensive team-building junkets abound. Why have a meeting in A.C./D.C. where 100% of attendees live within a fifty mile radius when you can go to the Bahamas for ten times the cost? No math competence, no conscience, no cares! It's money from the sky, for any Planner who dares!

Ike could hear them clearly, *"Not my dime so I can spend sublime,"* and he noticed that this refrain was sung throughout Central Planning offices in place of the "Pledge of Allegiance."

Ike often wondered how his workday compared to that of a Central Planner? Ike was busy every minute, time was money, profit was not a dirty word (greed was), and most everyone he worked with was trustworthy, diligent, and had a sense of duty to task. All were constantly measured on performance.

"What must it be like," he pondered, "To continually look over your shoulder at all of your fellow workers, wonder if they have made a deal behind your back, and know that every one of them is thinking the same thing?"

"What must it be like," he pondered, "To continually look over your shoulder at all of your fellow workers, wonder if they have made a deal behind your back, and know that every one of them is thinking the same thing?" It is management by committee, filled with paranoia, lacking accountability, and results in a vast, irresponsible spending of taxpayers' money.

None of this matters to a political Central Planner, who can stay in office forever. It is the brass ring of control and power sought with unrelenting effort, that they revere (personally and even with their foe) at any cost. "How foolishly shallow," Ike thought. "The Central Planners revere the ability of themselves or their foes to get elected/reelected no matter the means to do so. What a smarmy way to live!"

8 THE NEW CLASS

𝕴𝖐𝖊 was pleased with himself. He was contented because he knew he had the ability to clearly see things for what they were. He realized the difference between ideology and truth. Sometimes these two were aligned with each other, but it was rare. Ideology sounded fantastic, but the truth was usually far from it.

As Ike examined most of the original "pillars of society" he arrived at the same conclusion, time after time. The "Pillars" of family units, agriculture, business, immigration, education, media, arts/entertainment, and government all had many detrimental effects, especially when these entities were controlled by individual Central Planners or a Central Planning group.

Ike had read Henrik Ibsen's play, *Pillars of Society,* at a young age and perhaps this had some bearing on his thoughts and philosophy of life. The energetic intensity of Ibsen's play illuminated the effect of the "social lie," suffocated by provincialism. Consul Bernick (a main character) sells himself out for money and continually constructs lies to support his foibles. Central Planners are Consul Bernicks and it takes vision with acute interpretation to process their ruse. Merely seeing the "ink" is not enough. It must be seen through.

"There is nothing like observing for yourself, once you have the tools to dissect your observations," Ike thought. "I am pleased that I am able to do this but upset when I see the truth after the dissection of its opposing ideology. If only the Central Planners could be trusted."

Ike went further with his conclusions, "Many 'pillars' eventually cleanse themselves, much like nature does when it is harmed. I am skeptical that the greatest pillar (other than family), government, can do this. Central Planners have infested government to such an extent, causing the entitled to outnumber the producers. They cannot discern reality, they have no tools, they feel entitled to the producers' contributions and assets, and they re-elect the Planners who promise them the entitlements. A new class, the political class, has risen and replaced the middle class. This class is unctuous, growing daily (by design) and all-powerful. They have the characteristics of a giant squid – spewing rhetorical ink and backpedalling – all while gaining power."

At times, Ike wished he did not know these things; the veritable "out of sight, out of mind" was often desirable. Yet, if he kept this thinking, then he reasoned, "Am I worse than an entitled person, because I know the difference but take no action?" Ike grappled with the situation and then asked himself, "Would I rather be a pig satisfied or Socrates dissatisfied?" It was a question he had repetitively asked himself (and others) over his lifetime. "The pigsties are full and the swine seem to be enjoying themselves, but it is only temporary," he reasoned. "For isn't the quest to strive, know, learn, and create something far better than a request for entitlements?" "Yes!" was his resounding answer.

Ike's grandfather, Stanford Trueth, was a wise man. Stanford told Ike a story that is illustrative of numerous situations and widely applicable in several ways. The story was entitled – "Heedless Reality." Ike recalled his words almost verbatim:

On January 1ˢᵗ, a baby gobbler hatched, and began his life on Chopper Head's Turkey Farm. Let's call our newborn turkey Heed, which is short for Heedless. Heed was weak and his muscles were frail, but he managed to grow quickly and become quite strong in short order. All year, Heed romped on the farm, was fed twice daily so he did not have to forage for food, and was provided first class shelter. Life was good.

One of the donkeys, who lived in the barn, found Heed frolicking one day near the farm pond. The donkey's name was Wizeass, although he didn't look the part. Wizeass told Heed, 'You'd better keep your wits about you. The holidays are coming soon and life may not be so good for you as they approach.' The lazy turkey paid no heed and continued to stuff himself more each day…because the food was plentiful and he didn't have to work for it. Heed just knew this would go on forever. The day before Thanksgiving, Chopper paid a visit to the place where Heed and his friends were eating Chopper looked around and decided that Heed was the biggest and best turkey of the grounds. Heed looked tender. Chopper coaxed Heed with some corn, over near a block of wood. It was known as Chopper's block. Wizeass had

58

to turn away because he knew what was about to happen next.

Chopper placed some corn on the block, Heed strained his neck to grab a few kernels with his beak and WHACK!!! Chopper removed Heed's head with a cleaver. Heedless was now headless, and he reappeared on Chopper's Thanksgiving table the next day, plucked, basted, and cooked to perfection; fully consumed by the Chopper family.

Ike's perspicacity crystallized reality and he fully understood the gravity of this. His realization was that issues lacked complexity, especially ANY issue conferred by a Central Planner. "CONTROL by a Central Agency is dangerous and CONTROL that eradicates individual freedom is the most treacherous and perilous of all. THIS is the major issue," he realized. "There is now CONTROL of the media, agriculture, money and banking, education, and health care, by the supreme controllers, the Political Central Planners. The Central Planners have (pro)wrestled control of society's pillars and the destructive forces of this new political class will bring down this nation."

"Common sense tells me that it is impossible for the Central Planners to know what is best," Ike uttered under his breath. *"The breadth and depth of our country's people are as different as the desert is from a rain forest.* They could not possibly know nor do they really care what is best. If I completely ignore what my common sense tells me, mathematics verifies my argument anyway, and with the same conclusion. By the numbers alone, a few power brokers cannot possibly know what is best for this diverse population of 317 million people. Individual families, as cohesive units of solidarity, strong in their own belief systems, have a difficult time knowing what they desire. How could a Central Planner possibly know what millions of families want?"

He further reasoned, "Then again, if the power brokers, aka Central Planners, can CONTROL the majority of the population through their (pseudo) revered pillars, they can CONTROL the country. Simply transform the pillars, over time, and the meaning, values, ethics, and reverence that the pillars initially embodied will vanish and be superseded by opiate pillars of regulation and control."

Ike contemplated the original pillars and what they later became. He recognized the truth, and yet it was difficult for him to admit. "What about the majority who can no longer recognize the truth?" he posed. "And what about those like Dr. Nick, who comprehend the truth but reject it in favor of various rationalized justifications? There seem to be as many of the rationalizers as those who cannot recognize," he deduced.

He turned the pages of his personal notebook until a clean page appeared. With focused deliberation, he listed some key, original pillars and what they have now become:

FAMILY UNIT – once the backbone of societal equilibrium, now broken into bizarre and distorted fragments from its original, well-defined, balanced foundation.

"And what about those like Dr. Nick, who comprehend the truth but reject it in favor of various rationalized justifications?

AGRICULTURE/FOOD – transformed from multiplicities of small businessmen who earned their pay through hard work, perseverance, and determination; to a few major suppliers, tightly regulated, subsidized, and in many instances PAID for not working. The producers have become the opposite – they are NOT PAID for working, because taxes have consumed their income.

IMMIGRATION – Assimilated peoples, homogenized and blended with a defined goal of unity, have devolved to dissimilar cultures, each literally "carrying their own flag," and promoting a tribalistic mentality.

EDUCATION – once a disciplined, industrious institution with faculty and students possessing mutual respect and a shared mission for knowledge; to the present chaotic, undisciplined, programmed, socially engineered institution with "collectively unionized" faculty, while marching, protesting, and looking for their next intolerant, fabricated cause.

HEALTH CARE –originally managed by medical professionals, who had individual medical practices, with adequate time for diagnosis and treatment, now controlled by Central Planning: Censored and supervised by the Internal Revenue Service, and cemented to outlandish, never-ending, unrecognizable, impossible-to-follow, regulations and paper-work, which prevent proper medical attention because there is no time left to do so.

MONEY AND BANKING – currencies that were printed and backed by a gold standard (which had high value), now a fiat currency where monies are printed at the whim of Central Planners who own the banks into which the money is deposited and loaned to whomever they choose (mostly themselves), driving the national debt towards oblivion.

MEDIA - newspapers, radio, and television, once reliable as to accuracy and truth, to unreliable accuracy, constrained by political agendas which have become pillars of salt.

ARTS/ENTERTAINMENT – initially wholesome entertainment, respectful of individual and family values, to "anything goes" that portrays base, uncouth depictions of disrespectful thought, through art, TV, cinema, and "E-media," much of which is funded by Central Planners.

GOVERNMENT – initially created (by self-reliant, disciplined, purposeful, driven men) to have minimal input federally with most of the governance occurring locally, to a bloated, out-of-control Central Planning bureaucracy that is desperate to obtain ultimate CONTROL and POWER.

Ike carefully reviewed his notes. "Let me see," he mused. "If the Central Planners (maybe I should say "muggers"?) know what is best for all Americans, then why are things in such a shambles? They have had decades to work towards improvement, but the result is the exact opposite. The decay (from the original pillars' standards to their present status) had persisted too long and resulted in a stratified, fossilized, bureaucratic dust covered mess."

[He thought about his recent experience at the Chaos High School reunion when the entertaining leaders fawned for their roles in the school play. "Who was the central character that the major entertainers wanted to emulate? It was Delanno Ruse." Ike recalled. "Delanno pushed this country towards unsustainable entitlement programs with giant leaps of progressive dogma that thrust his "ruse" into the mainstream," Ike thought. "The young high school entertainers couldn't help themselves," he chortled. "Ego, spotlight, 'the cause,' and ignorance will be their demise," Ike summarized. This was the genesis for a future perfect storm of disaster because the embryonic proletariat was being comfortably incubated within replacement pseudo-pillars, skillfully fashioned by the Central Planners.]

9 CLASS REUNION

𝕿𝖍𝖊 special, long-awaited weekend had finally arrived: Ike's fiftieth high school reunion and the "Days of yore stories" were going to flow that evening. Ike knew everyone in his class of 315 students upon graduation, although that number had been currently reduced to 271. Fourteen percent had already passed away mainly because of the Vietnam War. Of the 271 remaining graduates, half were expected to attend; eighty percent were already retired. He was the youngest in his class by a full year but the difference in age now seemed miniscule. Most were close to seventy years of age. Ike was still working fifty hours per week, with no end in sight, running a company intimately involved with health care.

It was a public high school, but the graduates were top-notch. Even fifty years ago, 94% attended college upon graduation. He couldn't wait to see the Gumshoe Truth Seekers as a group, even though they had periodically kept up with one another throughout the years. There was Ike, (known to the "Gummers" as Gator – short for "Instigator") who spearheaded the group; Bat, whose real name was Barrett, had a two year old brother who couldn't quite pronounce

Barrett correctly, and "bat" came out of his mouth so it stuck; Worm, who always had his head in a book; and Goat, who would eat anything because he was always hungry.

Every Gumshoe had moved away from the area and each was looking forward to returning, albeit briefly. Some of the faculty were still alive and they planned to attend. Ike's high school experience had been a good one because the balance of discipline, teaching, learning, and

Ike's high school experience had been a good one because the balance of discipline, teaching, learning, and mutual respect of faculty, administration, and students was excellent.

mutual respect of faculty, administration, and students was excellent. Since this was the fiftieth anniversary, the festivities included a Saturday afternoon football game, a buffet from 6:00 pm – midnight, and a Sunday brunch at the superintendent's home from 11:00 am – 2:00 pm. For those who had interest, an invitation by the current administration was extended to attend the senior assembly on Monday.

Ike (Gator) gathered Bat, Worm, and Goat together at the brunch to decide if it would be worth attending the Monday assembly. He directed the Gumshoes' eyes to the invitation: Poor grammar and two misspelled words. They were astounded at the faux pas and it piqued their interest why these mistakes occurred. Worm had earned a PhD in English, eventually teaching graduate courses in literature, and in particular, was appalled by the errors. The Gumshoe Truth Seekers decided to attend the assembly to see all the "improvements to the school" the invitation had stated.

Overall, the festivities were fun and "Days of yore stories" reigned supreme. Intertwined throughout the merriment of the reunion, however, were common threads of incidents containing alarming stories about many peoples' children: Indicators of breakdowns in communication, in family ideals, in discipline, and in respect. The Gumshoes were quick to recognize the breakdowns and frequently compared notes. It was obvious that many of their friends had become poor parents resulting in incorrigible children with meaningless educations. The assembly instantly became the cause célèbre of the Gumshoes vis-à-vis the reunion.

Monday morning came and it was time to attend the senior assembly. As the Gumshoes arrived in the visitor's parking lot, Ike and his friends immediately noticed that their high school had been renamed to "CHS". They thought it was named after a local person of fame whom they did not recognize. If not, perhaps a word like "Central" was prefaced to "High School." They parked and slipped into the back of the gym where the assembly had just begun. A program was wadded up on the floor, so Ike picked it up and unraveled it. CHS stood for Chaos High School. What happened next was frightening.

It was week six of the new school year at Chaos High School. "*Spirits*" were high because senior class officers had been elected and this was the biggest occasion of the year to date. In fact, "spirits" were eternally high now-a-days at most schools. (The Gumshoes smelled it everywhere.) Meaningless proceedings were continually orchestrated by faculty and administration because these choreographed events resembled a concert and the students revered entertainment. Noise, clamor, irreverence, and feel good stuff helped control the majority of them. And why not? When one is well-schooled in Touchy Feely, Nebulosity, and History Redux, (all subjects now taught in year one, two, and three, respectively) illogical thought becomes the foundation for the way to live.

Ike and his friends had managed to see videos and read excerpts in the school paper about the class officers and their respective campaigns while attending the Sunday brunch at the superintendent's house. The administration was very proud of those seniors who aspired to "leadership" positions. Usually, these positions were the result of nothing more than a popularity contest.

Although there are two basic opposing sides that continually germinate within the American political system, what makes up the embryo, then eventually hatches, is a clone of its ancestors: Descendants that act, look, and perform exactly like their predecessors. These clones function as interchangeable "parts" within the political machinery and they blur so effortlessly that substitution is easily accomplished throughout the generations.

Names and faces are not important within this context. Actions are. Therefore, the characters and their names have been blurred over time, recurring again and again, becoming reincarnated as metaphors of themselves. The characteristic actions do not change, so the "Barq Parmas" and "Dubious Boshes" of the political world have been in existence forever. Whether two hundred years ago, one hundred years ago, or fifty years ago, these characters have now rematerialized in the twenty-first century as Hillib Hamrod, Dubious Bosh, Clint Billbong, etc!

The candidates for president of the class had been Clinton Billbong and Al Sore. Running for vice president was BidanJoe Hyman and Hillib Hamrod. Barq Pamma ran unopposed for treasurer. The candidates for secretary were Fancy Perosy and Antonio Fallace. Erigun Holster was unopposed for sergeant-at-arms.

Clinton Billbong (Clint, for short) whipped the masses into delightful emotions with cocktails of beautiful rhetoric. Yes, "spirits" were very high, even though no one inhaled! His moniker was yet to be uncovered, but what he learned in Touchy Feely 101 came in very "handy." His speeches were crafted down the hall in a large closet, and according to him, privacy was paramount while composing a message. The truth was another story. He was generally accompanied by an advisor and she helped boost his eloquence (and endorphins) to new heights. Clint was always spot on with his delivery.

Al Sore had a bad habit. Every speech was the same: "I will fight for you!" He was no match for Clint's "hands on" approach, and no one could figure out what Al Sore was fighting for. He positioned himself as "N'viroman," a superhero in the latest movie, and this seemed to help most students understand who he was, limited as their perspective was . Clint was clearly the superior squid with his folksy rhetoric and charm. Al just couldn't shake those silver spoons to get votes, and besides, he was so concerned with daily tap water temperatures you'd have thought he was a meteorologist, but that required judgment and knowledge of the sciences, neither of which he had.

In previous years, Al was the school basketball announcer and coined the phrase, "Nothing but NET" which, for a brief period of time, served him well. He even attempted to arrange a musical composition, "Internetzo", but it required too much talent and discipline to see it through. To no one's amazement, Clint won handily with landslide proportions for a high school election. Out of 315 seniors, Clint received 297 votes; Al garnered thirty three. Because math was no longer an important class within the school, no one noticed that there were more votes than voters even though seven students did not cast a ballot. Besides, even if someone did notice, Touchy Feely 101, Nebulosity 202, and History Redux 303 reduced everyone to a "mental mush" state. Moreover, the senior year's main class offering was PC 451 which finished them off. Very few recovered.

The race for vice president of the senior class was quite fanciful. BidenJoe Hyman portrayed himself as a "first time" candidate on his maiden voyage to victory. Hillib Hamrod was the toughest girl in school. She dressed in camo pants and tee shirts and her campaign manager was Jayne Flounder, who Hillib was very "fond of." Needless to say, no campaign manager was necessary but Jayne found a way to get her message across through Hillib.

Jayne was quite the exhibitionist; always wearing tank tops with actual depictions of ordinance flying toward a map of the U.S. BidenJoe Hyman ecstatically broke through first time status and won easily. Hillib and Jayne were too scary for the male students and thus, the election was decided. BidenJoe collected 112 votes; Hillib, thirty two. That meant 171 didn't vote. The V.P. position was the most meaningless of all offices, so no harm, no foul.

Barq Pamma was another matter. He was quite the campaigner, and ran unopposed for treasurer but spent four times the dollar amounts of all the other candidates combined, because he knew that "the more freebies, the more votes." He just couldn't help it! He loved to spend, especially when it was not his money. He was especially fond of purchasing unnecessary equipment and holding daily raffles.

Although unopposed, Barq eventually learned to print dollars on an unrestricted, hidden printer in his basement, and managed to convince everyone that the dollars were real, passing them out as favors (his picture was on both sides). There were no winners of these raffles but Barq and the voters did not seem to mind. In fact, no voter ever questioned this.

But perhaps Barq's greatest strength was that he could sway any audience. The teachers loved him and he received straight As in Touchy Feely, Nebulosity, and History Redux. In fact, he helped write some of the text for these classes and even wrote many questions on the tests. Yep, straight As and never studied.

When the votes were tallied, Barq received 160 votes, just a little over half. There were rumors that continually circulated about Barq but could never be proven. In fact, many things surrounding Barq could never be verified. It didn't matter to the students or faculty because Barq was a supreme rhetorical entertainer and theatrical oratory was highly esteemed, even deified at times. One oft repeated story was that Barq used a pen name to write out his thoughts and it was a clever way to communicate his philosophies with followers. Barq was never direct and this tactic allowed him to dodge issues and feign innocence. His pen name: Archy Toophis. There was hope he would change some day.

Another important race was Fancy Perosy versus Antonio Fallace for secretary of the senior class. Antonio a.k.a "Flash" Fallace, was a chauvinist in shark suit clothing. Naturally, he should be described first. Chauvinists have to be first; how ironic that he was campaigning against a female of all things. He was always hot dogging for the girls, especially girls he had never met. His summer job was driving the Oscar Meyer "Wiener" Van so he had some cash when school began, but quickly spent that on tailored clothes (always commando just in case), turtle necks, and beanie weenies, his favorite snack. In fact, Fallace's symbol was a beanie weenie.

Flash was politically savvy but had bad habits. One habit in particular would haunt him over his lifetime. His ego would flare up and Fallace was exposed for the sordid character he was. Let us not forget his facial appearance (physiognomy) coupled with his sincerity-rhetoric, an excellent combination for short term advances in his aspirations.

Then there was Fancy Perosy. She stuck to her talking points no matter what the subject or debate was. Logic had no place in her thinking. Antonio was easy meat for Fancy because she didn't have to think and the voters liked the consistent, repetitiveness of her responses. They thought her responses were meaningful because the replies were coming from Fancy. That's all they had to know. Remember, the students were filled with Touchy Feely and Nebulosity where logic cannot live. Fancy would say, "If you don't know I'm spoofing you now, you should elect me to see what I'm really about."

One favorite pastime of the students (besides tattooing one another) was entertainment. They adored entertainers and continually confused entertainers with leaders. They thought Fancy was a great performer

> *Once again, her repetitive response when asked to read minutes of the last meeting: "We will have to read the minutes to see what's in it."*

and thus a qualified leader. Fancy was an empty pants suit – a grandstander - so there was not enough substance to write about her, but she was entertaining enough to win secretary of the senior class. Her minutes of meetings were also very enjoyable reading but had nothing to do with those meetings. Once again, her repetitive response when asked to read minutes of the last meeting: "We will have to read the minutes to see what's in it." Incidentally, Fancy won going away: 232 votes to Flash's single digit (It was his vote for himself).

Lastly, Erigun Holster ran unopposed for Sergeant-At-Arms; a cake walk to victory. Erigun adored Barq and vice versa. When Barq began printing his own money for giveaway favors, some voters periodically became unruly because they thought their freebies weren't sufficient compared to what others had received. Barq calmed them with eloquence even though they were correct in their assessment. (This was a rather strange phenomenon because the voters couldn't reason otherwise, but freebies were involved and they knew a freebie when they saw one.)

Erigun always looked the other way in the face of truth. Barq just printed a little more money and gave it to Erigun: He was easy to buy. Antonio tried to align himself with this dynamic duo but three's a crowd and there was no room for a stiff like Flash. He retreated to a busy meat market in hopes of re-inventing himself with his individual moniker that would be instantly recognizable.

The class offices were filled with excellent entertainers, the faculty had their marching orders for Political Correctness 451* (PC 451). The entire assembly were in high spirits, and the stage was set for Poll Titian, CHS's principal for the last three years, to address the body politic, aka agents for change. Poll was filled with joy. He was the Central Planner of CHS. Course work and favors became the propaganda. It was a resounding success with the students.

A senior class, well schooled in Touchy Feely, Nebulosity, and History Redux, was prepared for Political Correctness 451, then on to either P.U. (Party University) or Spooph U. Poll exclaimed: "This moment makes me so proud! I am instructing the faculty to give all of you an A for the first six weeks of this new, school year." The students loved it! "We need to immediately begin work on the school play and put a lot of thought into who will be suited for the characters, so the next three weeks will be devoted to that before classwork begins. I insist on fairness so all auditions will be blind, behind a red curtain." There was more raucous applause from the assemblage.

Poll continued: "Nanny Stayet has partnered with I.D. Logg to produce a wonderful manuscript: *Our Hero – Delanno.* Every class officer stepped forward. They loved the drama and the moment. Each wanted desperately to be in the play. After all, each was a gifted actor/entertainer. Clint and Barq jumped to the podium with

Poll, waived to the crowd, joined hands, and hugged each another. Clint wanted to be Delanno Ruse, the play's central character, and immediately whispered this into Poll's ear. Poll smiled, an affirmative action that Clint would be chosen. Barq had his sights set on the Delanno part, but was beaten to the punch by Clint so he settled for Ellerby Jaye, a great supporting role to the Ruse, and he got the nod from Poll. (So much for fairness!)

Indeed, the stage was set. One final word was given from Poll Titian while delirium reigned, "I have published a calendar of all holidays, time off, and non-mandatory field trips for each of you. Please take one as you exit." It appeared that the students were hallucinating, their chant euphoric:

"From each according to his abilities, to each according to his needs!" It was their homework challenge to memorize this over the summer. Twelve words, one for each week of summer vacation.

Everything clarified for the on-looking Gumshoes, regarding the assembly and student behavior. Many parents from the Gumshoes' generation had shirked parenting duties and the Centrally Planned school became a food processer turned on high regarding the brains of the majority of students. The Gumshoes readily detected that the school's senior leaders' personalities were facsimiles of the previous generation's politicians, even replicating their duplicitous nature, looking and sounding like evolutionary reproductions.

Ike and his friends departed the assembly, speechless. Ike had always kept a little notebook and it became an invaluable reference for him to peer back in time to trace the social evolution of the entertaining Central Planners. The recapitulation was astounding. He opened a page of his notebook from his college days on which he had written: "A casual acquaintance, running for president of student body, placed signs all over campus, passed out roses, ran ads in

"From each according to his abilities, to each according to his needs!" It was their homework challenge to memorize this over the summer. Twelve words, one for each week of summer vacation.

school newspaper, got elected with 12% of students voting." Scratched in the margin with different colored ink was: "Made contacts and laid groundwork for future local, state, and national elections, and appointments." After college, Ike vividly recalled attending a mandatory, company-sponsored dinner for a gubernatorial candidate and turned to that page. "Says the right things, knows everyone, kisses the babies; always looking beyond the one shaking hands with, to the next groupie in line."

Ike always thought the election process was a charade, but sold to voters as, "You must vote because your vote makes a difference." He had written three pages of notes over the years dispelling this myth; example after example of why neither candidate of either party had made much of a difference, "fighting for you;" "preparing a better future for our children;" "deserving the American dream;" "improving education;" "protecting our borders;" "eradicating poverty," and "removing illicit drugs from our streets, schools, and playgrounds." All one has to do is read the newspaper and listen to a candidate chirp. It is repeated ad infinitum by every candidate. Their calumny put on an entertaining show for voters, fussing and debating issues, then meeting privately for dinner and drinks, afterwards. The only real worry of any candidate was how to get re-elected and most of them understood that well. If they failed, they became a lobbyist or reaped an appointment to a well-paying, meaningless job, portrayed as meaningful.

Ike recalled Gibbons's *The History of the Decline and Fall of the Roman Empire*, in which he wrote, "…Constantine too easily believed that he should purchase the favour of Heaven if he maintained the idle at the expense of the industrious, and distributed among the saints the wealth of the republic." (2) Constantine The Great, who ruled from 306-337 A.D., famous and revered by many throughout history, was a prime example of a "Central Planner." He thought he should "spread the wealth" which would buy favor from heaven. How dangerous, but there was nothing new with these personality types.

Over the centuries, names and faces changed but the need to control never changed. Taking other peoples' money to purchase favor from on high was beyond arrogant. Many historians believe that Constantine (who converted the Roman Empire to Christianity) used religion to enhance his stature, not vice versa. Constantine believed he knew best, ruled for thirty one years, and was a consummate Central Planner.

*Political correctness (PC) is deadly. Original thought, phrases, and expressive truths become replaced with malarkey, driven by fear of offending. Once it pervades a society, the society becomes controlled by it and the individuality of succinct, definitive expression disappears into an ink of tentative, nebulous absurdity. Isn't it odd that Central Planners' initials are the same as Political Correctness, just re-arranged (CP/PC)? Please refer to the short glossary of Political Correctness which verifies the farcicality of this tactic.

10 TRUTH OR CONSEQUENCES

𝕴t was now Friday the 13th, December 13th to be exact. The year: 2013. Ike was on his way to purchase some fresh calamari. One of his favorite avocations was cooking, and the evening's main course was to be freshly sliced, fried calamari. As he entered the seafood market, he was greeted by its owner, Verity Tempest, a long-time friend. (Verity had built her seafood business from scratch after receiving a degree in Meteorology). She always kept a weather radio on and today she had an alarmed look on her face. Before Ike could ask if there were a problem, Verity began removing seafood from the display shelves. She explained that some unusual storm clouds had formed from rare Pyrocumulus Clouds, and it was time to begin a "hunker down procedure," just in case severe weather ensued.

She was in quite a hurry, and left a few calamari on a display while closing the shop, apologizing for the rush and inability to serve him properly. Because Verity was not known to be an alarmist, Ike realized her due concern. So, he jumped back into his car and beat a hasty retreat to where he had built a safe haven with his fellow

Gumshoes. As he looked in the distance, there were huge black clouds unlike anything he had ever seen or studied. He recognized their menacing emergence and smiled, but it was a smile wrought from fear of the unknown scale of the impending perfect storm. "It is coming!" he proclaimed. "Truth is coming and it will be disastrous for a time. How long and to what extent, I do not know. But, I have prepared for it, no matter the severity."

Although his smile was marked with fearfulness, he was at peace with himself. He saw TRUTH; the only predator for a politician or Central Planner, on its way to cleanse the political environment. He had developed the tools to persevere with self-reliance. He had learned to distance himself from the Central Planners, and had maintained close friendships with those who had done the same. He realized there were going to be tornados of destruction, but the outcome would be a cleansing, resulting in a re-building of meaningful pillars, manifested in various ways. Lessons will be learned, as they have been throughout history, and then, eventually, another perfect storm will appear, to replicate the progression from idealism to truth.

> *He saw TRUTH; the only predator for a politician or Central Planner, on its way to cleanse the political environment.*

Ike had realized from an early age that nature was the purest form of life. It cleansed itself, knew what to do, and no corruption existed within nature's framework. What Ike did not understand until early adulthood was that most of humanity was corrupt; diametrically opposed to nature's purity. Nature dealt with everything and had no complaints while doing so. Humanity complained about everything and continually chose to ignore reality. Humanity is egocentric. Nature is altruistic.

Central Planners are humanity in its lowest forms; egocentric and corrupt. Ike concluded that because of these traits, there had always been corruption. It was unavoidable. He saw two potential solutions to this dilemma:

1. Remove as many responsibilities as possible from federal Central Planners, returning those responsibilities to local/state control. This solution might help temporarily, but local/state Central Planners would survive because they have become corrupt and dependent on federal Central Planners' goodies. This ensures federal C.P.s longevity. Ike debated this issue with many individuals and "term limits" was an answer from most of them. Ike concluded that term limits was not the answer because it

already existed at the ballot box. Any politician can be voted out of office. That IS the mechanism to limit the term. Ike realized that humanity is basically lazy and woefully uninformed politically. Charming rhetoric, woven with hope, repeatedly sealed humanity's fate. Ike concluded that removing responsibilities from Central Planners was not a solution because the Planners set things up so that this could not happen.

2. Become robust and innovative: Healthy, wealthy, and wise as the old saying goes. Do everything possible to avoid, rather than engage, Central Planners. This was contrary to what Ike had been taught in school, in the neighborhood, and by family. The hope of what the "sacred" right to vote implied was actually meaningless because humanity is corrupt. Therefore, the vote was one for continuance of corruption with a sugared overcoat of rhetorical hope. When Ike looked at the results of this sacred right he was astounded. Over time, the inherent corruption of humanity drives itself to political destruction, in various forms, periodically stabilizing, only to sink backwards from the sugared overcoat of rhetorical hope.

IKE'S CONCLUSION: Reality compels the logic of the healthy, wealthy, and wise approach. This approach is robust, enhances self-sufficiency, and rewards one's psyche, physicality, and emotional well-being, enriching the inner soul and fulfilling the experience of life. Become robust! Use ingenuity!

Ike was anxious for the storm to sweep in but he knew that the exact manner of the impact would be the storm's choice. Suddenly, without warning, as Ike lifted his face skyward, it began raining. He was now facing truth, feeling truth, and seeing truth. He was ready for the cleansing storm for it had been a severe drought for a very long time.

Dust had covered everything for so long, and it was a daily chore to keep things clean as the dust layer rapidly thickened.

(Two days previous, a butterfly had emerged from its cocoon, a thousand miles away, and flapped its wings, causing a slight shift of air current. This small, unnoticed event created enough force to lift a few microscopic grains of sand into the air, which grew as they attached to other grains. These grains became part of a thermal air current and were carried upwards to the edge of those Pyrocumulus Clouds into which they dropped, producing the rain that fell onto Ike's face.)

The rain was falling much harder by the minute, cleaning up the dust that the drought had caused. The winds picked up, and their increasing velocity helped hasten the cleansing. Ike called his Gumshoe buddies, one by one. Each recognized that the impending storm spelled disaster and all were prepared for it. The Gumshoes decided two years previously to build a large, remote, innovative, safe haven (bunker) for themselves and their wives. They named it "Animal House," stocked it with classical music, books, food, and water, and looked forward to their time together, riding out the inevitable storm. Bat, Worm, and Goat were now on their way to meet Ike in the bunker. Meanwhile, a few miles away from the bunker, Ike's home mailbox listed to the right, as the rain pelted it, cleansing the dust from its sides, revealing his name and address: Icanzee Trueth, #1 Reality Way. He climbed into the safe haven they used their ingenuity to think about and build, awaiting his buddies.

AFTERWORD

IKE'S SOLILOQUY– Ideology Springs Eternal Events ISEE

Over the years, Ike noticed that a major driver of human behavior in thought and deed is hope. Hope is a sibling of faith. Sooner or later, a person or group will turn to hope on most bothersome issues. Central Planners are masters at understanding this and they exploit hope to sway people to vote for them, using their ideology as a "carrot." The "stick" would be the awful consequences that would result if the Central Planner were not elected/re-elected. Hence, the carrot and the stick are interwoven throughout a C.P.'s fabric and they are rhetorical artists at manipulating this tactic to fit their ideology and enable their ability to remain in office. Hope feels good and is a wonderful alternative to reality. Followers of Central Planners become so enamored with them that they erect statues, construct libraries, commission portraits, build bridges, name buildings, streets, fountains, and plazas for them, and write biographies of their lives. Hope is so strong for an ideological follower that reality has no consideration in their thought process. The same is true for the entitled who now exceed 50% of the electorate. Ike recalled a few major "hopes" of recent history leading to the present:

> *Followers of Central Planners become so enamored with them that they erect statues, construct libraries, commission portraits, build bridges, name buildings, streets, fountains, and plazas for them, and write biographies of their lives.*

FDR's - The New Deal –*The main lesson we have learned from the New Deal is that wholesale government intervention can -- and does -- deliver the most unintended of consequences. This was true in the 1930s, when artificially high wages and prices kept us depressed for more than a decade, it was true in the 1970s when price controls were used to combat inflation but just produced shortages. It is true today, when poorly designed regulation produced a banking system that took on too much risk.(5)*

The Great Society and The War On Poverty – **no matter who's statistics one reads, today, there are 45 to 50 million individuals within the United States mired in poverty after the "war on poverty" was declared fifty years ago by President Lyndon Johnson, and over one trillion dollars spent. President Johnson's exact words, taken from his first state of the union address, January 8, 1964:**

For my part, I pledge a progressive administration which is efficient, and honest and frugal. The budget to be submitted to the Congress shortly is in full accord with this pledge.

It will cut our deficit in half -- from $10 billion to $4,900 million. It will be, in proportion to our national output, the smallest budget since 1951.

It will call for a substantial reduction in Federal employment, a feat accomplished only once before in the last 10 years. While maintaining the full strength of our combat defenses, it will call for the lowest number of civilian personnel in the Department of Defense since 1950.

This budget, and this year's legislative program, are designed to help each and every American citizen fulfill his basic hopes -- his hopes for a fair chance to make good; his hopes for fair play from the law; his hopes for a full-time job on full-time pay; his hopes for a decent home for his family in a decent community; his hopes for a good school for his children with good teachers; and his hopes for security when faced with sickness or unemployment or old age.

So, therefore, I recommend legislation authorizing the creation of a tripartite industry committee to determine on an industry-by-industry basis as to where a higher penalty rate for overtime would increase job openings without unduly increasing costs, and authorizing the establishment of such higher rates.

Democracy in Iraq – President George Bush believed in democracy, so much so, that he felt the Iraqi people should have a democracy. (We in America are a Republic, not a democracy.) His words from a speech, November 19, 2003, given in London: *We did not charge hundreds of miles into the heart of Iraq and pay a bitter cost of casualties and liberate 25 million people only to retreat before a band of thugs and assassins. We will help the Iraqi people establish a peaceful and democratic country in the heart of the Middle East.* On August 26, 2003 stated in his remarks to the 85th American Legion Convention, President Bush reiterated: *Iraq's progress toward self-determination and democracy brings hope to other oppressed people in the region and throughout the world. It is the rise of democracy that tyrants fear and terrorists seek to undermine. The people who yearn for liberty and opportunity in countries like Iran and throughout the Middle East are watching and they are praying for our success in Iraq.*

Shouldn't the people of Iraq decide their government as we decided ours? Maybe they would choose a monarchy, not a democracy.

Eleven years after hoping for democracy in Iraq, bolstered by America's military, the country is in a total shambles with terrorists consuming the land, executing thousands of Iraqi soldiers and countrymen in their march for control of Iraq.

Health Care for All! – President Barack Obama, operating under his signature wish statement (hope and change), with backing by a partisan majority in Congress, signed the Affordable Care Act. Its hope was health care for all. Its reality was unintelligible policy and mix of words with too many unintended consequences to list. Even the Speaker of the House, Nancy Pelosi, who had not read the legislation, remarked with great glee - *But we have to pass the bill so that you can find out what is in it.*

President Obama - *...I am absolutely certain that generations from now, we will be able to look back and tell our children that this was the moment when we began to provide care for the sick and good jobs to the jobless; this was the moment when the rise of the oceans began to slow and our planet began to heal; this was the moment when we ended a war and secured our nation and restored our image as the last, best <u>hope</u> on earth. This was the moment -- this was the time -- when we came together to remake this great nation so that it may always reflect our very best selves and our highest ideals.*

Ike noticed that most people would rather live outside of reality, ("happy land") than face it. Happy land feels good, is touchy feely, has many grey areas, rewrites history, is politically correct, is non-committal, doesn't require discipline, affects all levels of intellect, is spoon-fed, and eventually alters their world view, obstructing truth. Happy land is easy; truth and reality can be difficult. Medication can help transport you to happy land if you prefer its pseudo, utopian cultivations, and that has happened nationwide. Pop a pill, elevate your mood, and reality goes away

> *...this was the moment when the rise of the oceans began to slow and our planet began to heal...*

A Central Planner's intentions may be honorable but the results of his actions are the same as if he were dishonorable. A Central Planner's actions remove the right of an individual (or group) to fail, by replacing that right with what he deems is best for the individual or group. In this sense then, a Central Planner is a malevolent dictator who presents himself as a benevolent one. Is it not worthwhile to allow humanity the individual freedom to fail versus imposing slavery on humanity to a perceived success because somebody thinks it so? Is it not better for one to be free, learn from failure, then strive to overcome that failure, than to become enslaved to a Planner who believes he knows what is best for you, because your will to strive has been removed by him? The tragic result of this situation is nothing more than a continual decay of the enslaved for the benefit of the enslaver.

The political class has expanded from the public sector into the private one by suffocating individual uniqueness...

Ike had always known, "The smallest gift in the universe is someone who is wrapped up in himself." "What better definition than that of a Central Planner," he concluded

The political class, encouraged by the Oz of Central Planners, has expanded from the public sector into the private one by suffocating individual uniqueness through its tools (education, media, political correctness, creating new pillars, re-writing history, etc.), and controlling freedom through fear, regulations, procedures, agencies, and laws. The free marketplace is choked to death by the public sector Central Planners whose strangling tactics are so pervasive that the solution to their stifle as well as the primary escape route for the private, free marketplace is a robust, self-sufficient location using individual innovation, while awaiting the devastation of the Planners' self destruction.

And the rains persisted, washing the years of stratified, fossilized, bureaucratic dust from the landscape, cleansing, purifying, and purging as it fell.

IKE'S CURIOUS BUNKER SIGN

Ike had a curious looking sign at the entrance of his bunker. It is depicted below and the other Gumshoes knew what it meant.

It is a cuneiform inscription; the earliest known written appearance of the word *freedom* (amagi), or *liberty*. This word was taken from a clay document written about 2300 B.C. in the Sumerian city-state of Lagash. Sumerian was spoken in southern Mesopotamia, (modern day Iraq) and cuneiform is the earliest known writing system, originating to about 3500 B.C. Cuneiform means "wedge shaped" because the strokes were made from pressing stiff reed tips into soft clay that later hardened. Ike often wondered if this was written by a scribe who was weary of being oppressed and mentally tormented by a Central Planner.

ABBREVIATED GLOSSARY of POLITICAL CORRECTNESS

LOGOCRACY is the rule of, or governance by, words.
POLITICAL CORRECTNESS is the rule by correct terminology.
Combine these "rules" and they become weapons of Central
Planners. Here are just a few to illustrate P.C.'s absurdity.

Baa Baa Rainbow Sheep – Baa Baa Black Sheep

Differently Logical – Wrong

Factually Unencumbered – Ignorant

Freedom Fries (In France) – French-fried potatoes

*Ho-Ho-Ho – Use your imagination on why Santa Clauses in Sydney,
Australia were banned from saying this.*

Involuntarily Leisured – Unemployed

Nasally Repetitive – Snore

Negative Saver – Spendthrift

Newcomer – Immigrant

Nondiscretionary Fragrance – Body Odor

Personal Access Unit – Manhole

Speedy Transmission of Near-Factual Information – Gossip

Spring Spheres – Easter eggs

Unsavory Character – Criminal

A FIELD GUIDE SUMMARY OF CENTRAL PLANNERS

I Think, Therefore It Is: Central Planners do not think often and obviously not deeply. Otherwise, our country would not be in the mess it is in. They have staffs (friends and relatives) that think and do for them. C.P.s travel around to look good and they love photo ops. Beware of their sojourns and "everywhere" photos.

I Know What Is Best For You: Of course they do! They are special selections placed on "narrow" ballots and elected by emotional voters, therefore, they "just know." It is a magical knowledge because they are special.

Reelect Me Because I Represent Your Hopes And Dreams: I magically know and I can help all of you.

This Is A Complicated Situation: So complicated that it takes a magical leader who magically knows what to do – give speeches, organize committees, ensure studies.

This Is A Complex World We Live In: Magical leadership is needed to help all of us through our complex world and its problems, solved by more speeches, committees, and studies, which never accomplish anything, but sound marvelous, initially.

We Worked Very Hard: Long into the night (for show) I worked, to solve the problem, for you.

Never Answer A Question: use beautiful rhetoric with humble dance steps to sway the audience away from truth.

Use Hope Consistently: the word "hope" diverts reality to ideology; truth and logic simply disappear.

Act Belligerent, Cantankerous, And Argumentative: When "accosting" the opposition or making a point to help, understand this tactic fully.

Continually Work On The Knife Smile: Know how to smile beautifully while stabbing your prey in the back with a rhetorical, serrated machete.

Manipulate The "I Did" Subliminal Maneuver: When asked any question, continually insert "I did goodies for you," into the sentence.

Embellish Or Plagiarize: What ever it takes to enhance stature.

Know How To Find Money: Money for reelection and constituents is an absolute necessity for survival.

Use The Media Incessantly: Manipulate the media for positive recognition.

Avoid Paying Taxes: No taxes, more in-pocket money. Simple!

Write Loophole Laws For Donators: How else to prove love?

Artful Creation Of The Scandal: If all else fails, get as dirty as possible; invent a scandal.

Say Anything, Do Nothing: Manipulate words to augment hope; use the word – "future" whenever possible.

Avoid Logic: Replace with emotion, straw men and non sequiturs.

FOOTNOTES

(1)F.A. Hayek, *The Road To Serfdom, 1944*

(2)Edward Gibbon, *The Decline And Fall Of The Roman Empire – Vol 1.*

*(3)*Journal Of The American Medical Association, *311(8), 806-814, Prevalence of childhood and adult obesity in the United States, 2011-2012*

*(4)*Katharine O. Seelye, New York Times, February 4, 2010, *Health Care's Share of U.S. Economy Rose at Record Rate*

(5) How Government Prolonged the Depression, Wall Street Journal, Harold L. Cole and Lee E. Ohanian, February 2, 2009, Mr. Cole is professor of economics at the University of Pennsylvania. Mr. Ohanian is professor of economics and director of the Ettinger Family Program in Macroeconomic Research at UCLA.

INDEX

ABOUT THE AUTHOR

Michael Webb is a results-oriented businessman who currently runs a health care benefits management company. Forty six years of hands-on experience and observation, utilizing his knowledge and ability at all levels of business, nationally and internationally, have provided an ample framework for his skills, analyzing key issues. He is a registered pharmacist, a graduate of the University of Kentucky, College of Pharmacy and lives in Greenville, SC.

Made in the USA
Lexington, KY
06 September 2014